DID NELSON TURN
A BLIND EYE?

NELSON AND THE ROYAL NAVY

FASCINATING FACTS AND
EVERYDAY PHRASES EXPLAINED

Peter Ryding

PATHFINDER

Published by Pathfinder Partners Ltd.

ISBN 0-9551525-2-6
ISBN 978-0-9551525-2-8

© Peter Ryding 2006

Designed by Oxford Designers & Illustrators

Cover design by Baseline Arts Ltd., Oxford

Illustrated by Chris Rothero

Printed and bound in Germany by GGP Media GmbH, Pößneck

I must thank Louise, Edward and Richard, who have encouraged me throughout the WINKT project and without whose support it would never have got off the ground.

However, this special edition of the 'Well I Never Knew That' series is dedicated to my father, Ralph John Ryding, who dodged the Atlantic wolfpacks in the Second World War; and to Lord Nelson and all the other members of the Royal Navy who have risked, or lost, their lives to protect Great Britain.

PR

Acknowledgements

I would like to take this opportunity to thank everyone who has so enthusiastically embraced and supported the WINKT project from its inception: the many dinner guests who have patiently listened, challenged and in some cases politely fallen asleep whilst I have shared my latest linguistic discoveries; Steve, the guy in the pub who challenged me to write the first book; Peter at ODI, who has been a stalwart supporter and always kept a sense of humour despite everything (and there have been lots of 'things'!); Chris, my artist, who has kept going through the crazy requests that I have made of him; Gillian, who has challenged and checked and added her own ideas despite an apparently endless set of iterations.

Of the many others, who are too many to fit on one page but who have encouraged me throughout, I would like to thank Crisspy the Duck and his friends, Simon, Neil, Spence, Tim (Nadia), Sam (Jo), Hutch, Gordon, Alexander The Great and Henry V, all of whom have played their roles, plus the designer of the keel of the boat, without whom we would all have drowned.

Also thanks to the many members of WINKT the club who continue to write in with both intriguing questions and fascinating discoveries.

Thanks to every one of you.

Contents

Foreword

Lieutenant Commander
Frank Nowosielski MBE Royal Navy,
Commanding Officer, HMS Victory

Two hundred years ago off the coast of Spain, Lord Nelson and the British fleet won a famous victory, which confirmed the Royal Navy's supremacy at sea. That decisive victory at the Battle of Trafalgar on 21 October 1805 once and for all put paid to Napoleon's plans to invade Britain and set the stage for the expansion of the British Empire.

This heritage has had a massive impact upon our stature in the world – and, perhaps more surprisingly, upon our language.

As Commanding Officer of HMS *Victory* I feel privileged to write this foreword from the ship where Admiral Lord Nelson spent the last two years of his life, and planned and commanded the Battle of Trafalgar. Despite a lifetime's service within the Royal Navy, even I have been surprised at the fascinating and intriguing background to many of the words and phrases that are in common use today. This book will take you on a voyage of discovery through their derivations – some hilarious, some grim and bloody, and many of them evocative of our nation's proud and colourful history.

So get a tot of 'Nelson's blood' and 'splice the mainbrace', while you read and enjoy this remarkable adventure story of how Nelson, the Battle of Trafalgar and the Royal Navy have enriched our history and become part of our everyday language. You may feel 'groggy' in the morning but I am sure that you will smile and say – 'WELL, I NEVER KNEW THAT!'

Lt Cdr Frank Nowosielski

Preface

Imagine you are a foreigner who has just learnt the basics of the English language. You proudly walk into a room of native English speakers and listen to their conversation.

'Was it a cock-up you ask? I should bally say so! But it's a good job he had an extra string to his bow because they had him running from pillar to post in that job. His boss's ideas were so off the wall that it wound him up something proper. No wonder he's legged it!'

You may well think you had been on the wrong course!

But it's not just the phrases we use that make English tough to learn and a joy to use. Our language has absorbed more subtleties and richness from other nations than any other. Indeed, English is by far the most widely used official language in the world. We also have the largest vocabulary in the world, at over 250,000 words in the *Oxford English Dictionary*. Having said that, we each tend to pick from our own favourite 2–3,000 most of the time, rarely stepping outside our comfort zone. To put this into context, Shakespeare used over 21,000 words and a top scrabble player will know over 80,000 words!

So, with all this richness and precision at our fingertips, such that we can intuitively distinguish between a simple 'room' and a grander 'chamber' (in a way that many languages cannot), what do we do? We dredge up obscure phrases that often arose for reasons that are no longer relevant and that people don't really understand anyway. Or, even worse, ones that they misunderstand. For example, imagine the foreigner who overhears that something is 'cheap at half the price'. What does that mean? Is it saying that it would be cheap if it was half the current price? In other words, that it is expensive? Or is it saying that it is cheap because it is half the price you were expecting to pay? If *we* are not sure – what chance do foreigners have?

In many cases phrases have simply gone wrong over the ages. For example, take 'the exception that proves the rule'. Pardon? Are we saying that finding an exception to a rule somehow proves that the rule is correct? Surely that has to be utter tosh!

It is only through patient research and an understanding of our heritage that we can make sense of such expressions. In this case the explanation goes back to the Normans' invasion of England in 1066 and their desire to have a clear set of rules with which they could govern the country. The trouble was that the barely literate Anglo-Saxons had few written laws. Most were simply 'known' to those who dispensed justice. However, the Normans passed a law that said that if someone could prove beyond doubt that there was an exception to a law, then by implication that would prove, in another case, that the law did exist. For example, a trader who had a pass allowing him to travel at night after the curfew hour – literally, the hour at which the fire (*feu*) had to be covered (*couvert*) – would prove that the law of curfew did exist. This in turn would enable the

prosecution of someone who broke the curfew. Hence, an exception to a rule does not in fact prove that the rule is correct. However, it does prove that the rule exists!

Yet another example of things going wrong is the phrase 'Don't spoil the ship for a hap'orth of tar!' Now, tar may be cheap, but a hap'orth (that's half a penny's worth for those born after 1980) of it does not go far when you are trying to waterproof an entire ship! In fact, by digging into the past we discover that the saying originally referred not to a ship at all but rather to a humble *sheep*! The reason is that just about the only help you could give a sheep with an open sore or wound was to slap on a dollop of tar. This would at

least close the wound and was of course worth doing – especially given the financial value of sheep in medieval days, when they produced the vast majority of England's income. After all, without them we could not have afforded to fight the French through the Hundred Years War! And let's face it, you don't often get the chance to humiliate the entire French nation like we did at the battles of Crécy, Poitiers and Agincourt! Well worth a hap'orth of tar so that we don't spoil the *sheep*!

However, the story is not all mistakes and misunderstandings. Some derivations are a sheer joy to discover. Like the Greek god who used to jump out on humans and scare them away

from his personal harem of nymphs and dryads. His name was Pan, from which we get the word PANIC! Or the need for sailors to be flogged up on the main deck because down below in the cramped conditions there was NOT ENOUGH ROOM TO SWING A CAT – o' nine tails! Why nine tails? Because the Royal Navy decided that the normal three-headed scourge representing the Father, the Son and the Holy Ghost was not 'holy enough' for wicked sailors and so created a 'trinity of holy trinities'. Hence nine tails that left deep scratches on the skin just like the claws of a CAT. And of course the scars would then stay with the troublemaker for the rest of his life, making him a MARKED MAN!

There is also the wonderful realization that so often when different words sound similar they are in fact the same word,

or at least come from the same original source. For example, cheque books, checkmate in chess, checklists, rain checks, the checks (bills) you get in American restaurants, the game of chequers, checkered patterns, the Chancellor of the Exchequer, Chequers pub signs, the prime minister's country house Chequers and simply 'checking something out', all derive from medieval military coups in Persia! Wonderful!

Having studied our language hand in hand with our history for over two decades, I am still surprised, amazed and delighted at what treasures I uncover on a regular basis. Creating this series of books has been a massive and painstaking undertaking, bringing a lot of pleasure and at times a lot of frustration. I just hope that you have fun with the books and that you will find something fascinating, insightful and intriguing within each book that makes you say 'Well, I Never Knew That!' And of course, when you do, please tell your friends and join WINKT the club at www.winkt.com – and vote for WINKT to become a new word in the English language! Thank you for doing so.

Don't just enjoy the English language – CREATE IT!

How to use this book

This book has been written in a unique format so that you can enjoy it in several different ways:

1. You can **read it cover to cover** as an adventure into the rich stories and interconnectedness behind our language.

2. You can **flick to a page** and discover fascinating facts bit by bit.

3. You can **study the pictures** at the start of each chapter and try to work out the sayings that await you inside.

4. You can **seek out specific words** and sayings via the index.

5. You can **use it as a quiz book** on your own or spoken out loud with friends, by reading each paragraph and then stopping just before the CAPITALS reveal the answers.

6. You can just leave it in the loo for everyone to enjoy. But beware – your guests may not come out for some time! And, of course, when they do they are bound to say – **'Well, I Never Knew That!'**

1

Nelson's Navy

Life at the end of the 18th century was pretty
tough for most people – but in Nelson's navy it was
tougher still. The work was gruelling, the discipline
harsh, and battle a grim and grisly business. Today
we still use the language of the paupers, criminals
and pressed men who populated
His Majesty's warships.

Well, I never knew that . . .
. . . if you don't know the ropes, you can't go larking around

Being a sailor in Nelson's era was a complex and dangerous job. Not only did sailors have to be able to balance and work on the constantly moving decks, they had to know how the rigging worked and be ready to climb up to the sails whatever the weather. When they were familiar with all this they would KNOW THE ROPES. When a young sailor was beginning his career, a more experienced sailor would SHOW HIM THE ROPES – a phrase we still use to mean teaching someone how something works by doing it, rather than through a textbook or written instructions.

The fittest and most experienced sailors would be used to trim the very highest sails. This was skilled and dangerous work, especially in bad weather. The nickname given to these sailors is still used as a compliment to someone whom you admire: TOP MAN.

During times of inaction young sailors would often race each other up to a crow's nest and out to the end of a yardarm and back down again. This was tolerated by the officers because it provided entertainment for the crew and honed skills needed in emergencies. From the Old English word for play, *lac*, it became known as LARKING AROUND. When the race involved going to the very top of the mast – near the sky – it was called SKYLARKING.

Lobre is old English for a lumbering, clumsy oaf. Sailors used this term to describe a landsman who has just joined a crew at sea and is consequently unstable on his feet and in the rigging: a LANDLUBBER. During the Napoleonic wars many landlubbers were press-ganged into the navy. In comparison the experienced sailors were called ABLE SEAMEN.

In early galleons the toilets were usually at the front of the galleon near the figurehead. This is where the junior crew lived and at the opposite end from the captain's quarters. Hence the nickname for toilets at sea, THE HEADS.

Well I never knew that . . .
. . . showing a leg could lead to the son of a gun

Women were allowed to sleep on board ships in harbour. However, the men still had to perform their duties and keep to the usual 'watch' system. So officers would do the rounds of the hammocks and, if they noticed someone in a hammock who was not getting up, would ask them to show what sex they were by putting a leg outside. If it was a smooth woman's leg, the sleeper could stay abed; if it was a hairy man's leg, the sailor had to get up. The instruction was SHOW A LEG or SHAKE A LEG.

Superstitious sailors thought that having women on board ships at sea was bad luck; still, prostitutes would often come aboard in port and then stay there in hiding until the ship was well out to sea. A woman who subsequently had a baby would be forced to have it between the guns, perhaps behind a sheet to provide some semblance of modesty. Given that the father was often difficult to identify, the child (if male) would be recorded as being a SON OF A GUN – a description now used to suggest that someone has a mystery or surprise in his past.

Most sailors lived very rough-and-ready lives but still believed that they needed a proper burial to go to heaven, and that meant having the money to pay for it. But there was always the risk of money being lost or stolen; so the canny sailor would have a large gold ring put into his ear.

Again to ensure he would get a proper Christian burial, every sailor wanted to ensure that even if he was killed and his body badly damaged during a fight or shipwreck, it could still be correctly identified. So when sailors came across a Tahitian religious custom called the *tatu*, they adopted it as a form of distinctive identification: the TATTOO.

Well, I never knew that . . .
. . . Nelson got us all pickled

After the Battle of Trafalgar Nelson's body was placed in a large barrel of brandy to preserve it on the journey back to Britain. Many people thought it was rum, giving the Royal Navy its nickname for rum, NELSON'S BLOOD. This method of preservation also gave us a phrase meaning to get drunk, to GET PICKLED, as well as reviving an older expression, AS DRUNK AS A LORD.

At the Battle of the Nile in 1798, another of Nelson's famous victories, *L'Orient*, the flagship of the French navy, was pulverized by the British fleet. The admiral of the French fleet, Brueys, had his legs blown off and was propped up in a barrel so that he could keep fighting until eventually he bled to death. The ship's captain, Louis Casabianca, was also killed and the ship was ablaze, on the point of sinking. Yet the captain's son, a 12-year-old trainee officer, refused to leave his father's side and famously went down with the ship. Hence the phrase TO REMAIN ON THE BURNING DECK, meaning to remain resolute despite knowing you will suffer terrible consequences. The incident was captured both in a painting and in a poem called 'Casabianca' by Felicia Hemans:

> *The boy stood on the burning deck,*
> *Whence all but he had fled*
> *The flame that lit the battle's wreck*
> *Shone round him o'er the dead.*

In fact, the flames on the blazing ship reached the powder room just before it sank. The resulting explosion was so loud that the whole battle stopped and silence fell for several minutes.

Some management consultants use an adapted phrase to illustrate that a management team must feel an urgent and immediate danger to their current situation before they decide to undergo a major change: that they won't shift until they are on a BURNING PLATFORM.

The size and quality of fighting ships were assessed primarily by the number of guns they had on board: for example, a ship with between 2 and 20 guns was defined as sixth-rate, one with 21–40 guns as fifth-rate, while two-deckers with 64–74 guns were called third-raters. The biggest ships, which had 100 or more guns on three decks, were awesome in their size and fighting ability. HMS *Victory*, Nelson's flagship at the Battle of Trafalgar in 1805, was one such ship. It had 104 guns, many of which could fire a 32-pound cannonball up to 2 miles. In fact, the *Victory* alone had more firepower than all the British cannons at the Battle of Waterloo. These ships were so impressive – by far the biggest moving objects the world had ever seen – that their title became associated with the very best of anything: FIRST RATE. By definition, anything that is not as magnificent or impressive is SECOND RATE.

Naval tactics in Nelson's day involved the ships of each fleet lining up one in front of the other, then sailing alongside the enemy line of ships so that each line could fire at the ships opposite it. This mode of fighting, called 'line of battle', required sturdy ships to withstand the barrage of cannon fire, and a ship that was rated and could therefore take part in the line of battle was called a SHIP OF THE LINE.

Well, I never knew that . . .
. . . it was dangerous to accept a drink from the King

Recruitment for the army and navy in past centuries could be a very crude affair. Up to the 17th century each ship's captain had been responsible for recruiting his own crew. Eventually, however, Britain's requirement for a strong and effective navy to protect its growing trade and overseas colonies meant that there was a shortage of sailors, and new ways of attracting – or persuading – men into the navy had to be found. Money was, not surprisingly, the most effective draw: so a new recruit would be paid a small loan or his initial wage in advance, and

in return he engaged himself to serve in the Royal Navy for many years. Thus joining the navy – or, indeed, the army – was known as TAKING THE KING'S SHILLING.

However, it still wasn't easy to get enough new sailors to volunteer, so more devious methods came into play. If a recruiting officer could get a man physically to take a shilling from him, he could claim that he had accepted the money as pay and so had committed himself to the King's service. A favourite trick was to buy a man a drink of beer, served in a pewter tankard, and drop a shilling in it. The target would not see the shilling until he had finished his ale – at which point it was claimed that he had accepted payment (the coin) and the King's hospitality (the beer) and had thus signed up to the Crown's service. At this point he would be forcibly taken off to the ship in question. Often this would result in brawls as the 'recruit' and his friends tried to evade the recruiters – indeed, the whole process frequently descended into thuggery, with squads of burly armed sailors grabbing men from pubs or even from merchant ships. The name given to this approach, from the French word for 'to lend', *prêter*, is still used to imply that someone has been coerced into an action or PRESS GANGED.

Some of the legislation that enabled the pressing of men has actually never been repealed – although by the middle of the 19th century pay and conditions had improved to the point where the number of volunteers was enough to keep the navy supplied with manpower. Incidentally, the practice of tricking people by dropping a coin in their beer is what led to the invention of the GLASS-BOTTOMED TANKARD – so that you can check before you start drinking that you are not about to accept the 'King's shilling'.

The press gangs were not just a European phenomenon. At the end of the 19th century on the west coast of America, many people got drunk on hospitality offered by sea captains

only to wake up to a hangover and the awful discovery that they were on a boat headed for the Far East as a pressed crewman. Many of these ships plied a route to and from China, using the port of Shanghai; so men caught by this trick were said to have been SHANGHAID.

Well, I never knew that . . .
. . . Queen Elizabeth I named the First World War's battleships

It was in the ninth century, to combat the incessant attacks by Vikings from Scandinavia, that King Alfred the Great established England's first ROYAL NAVY.

In the 17th century the British fleet was split into three squadrons, each having its own version of a flag showing the cross of St George with the Union flag in the top corner near the flagpole. These flags were called the RED, BLUE AND WHITE ENSIGNS. However, in 1864 these squadrons were abolished and the flags reassigned: the red was given to the MERCHANT NAVY, the blue to the AUXILIARY NAVY and the white to the warships.

The royal toast to the monarch is traditionally made with everyone standing up. However, when King Charles II, returning from his exile in Holland in 1660, rose for the toast on board ship he banged his head: so he instructed that, from then onwards, senior officers in the Royal Navy could TOAST THE MONARCH SITTING DOWN. Since then the privilege has been extended to all officers in the Royal Navy and Royal Marines when dining in their mess – and it still applies, even on land. However, if anyone who is not a naval officer is present, that person does not have the dispensation and therefore, out of courtesy, everyone does stand for the toast.

In 1797 an attempted mutiny was defeated when the Royal Welch Fusiliers refused to join in and issued a communication declaring their undying loyalty to the King, George III. In his appreciation, the King declared that the regiment no longer needed to prove their fidelity by making the loyal toast. To this day the only time they toast the monarch is on St David's Day, and they sit while they do so. They then continue to sit through the National Anthem.

During the 19th century the apparent barbarity of discipline in the Royal Navy led to Queen Victoria imposing a highly visible and embarrassing punishment on all naval officers – which became a rule that is still applied to this day. They are forbidden to attach their ceremonial swords to their belts and so always have to CARRY THEIR SWORDS IN THEIR LEFT HANDS.

All UK armed forces originally saluted with the palm showing, to make clear that they held no concealed weapon. However, the scars and rope burns on the palms of sailors prompted Queen Victoria to request that they conceal their palms when saluting. This is why the Royal Navy salutes differently from the army, showing the back of the hand instead of the palm.

During Queen Elizabeth I's reign the Royal Navy built several new ships with bold names such as *Revenge, Redoubtable* – and

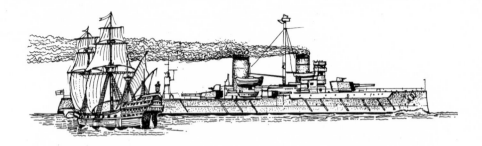

another chosen to make the crew feel brave and resolute. This name continued to be used as an individual ship's name. When Britain made the world's most powerful and awesome warship just before the First World War it gave the vessel this name. Other ships of the same design also generically took the same name. That name, meaning 'fear nothing', was DREADNOUGHT.

Up until the late 18th century ships in the Royal Navy were referred to just by their individual names, for example *Royal Sovereign*. At about this time admirals and other writers

unofficially began to refer ingratiatingly to the King's ownership of all the navy's vessels. A shortened version of the full phrase was first used in 1789, attached to the ship *Phoenix*. Within 30 years it had become official practice to prefix any ship's name with HMS, STANDING FOR 'HIS MAJESTY'S SHIP'. Of course, handily the same initials can also stand for *Her* Majesty's Ship! **WINKT!**

2

A Sailor's Life

Whether out of poverty, patriotism or
ambition, thousands of England's young men
went to sea in Nelson's heyday. Their life had a
language all its own – and it has seeped
right through ours.

Well, I never knew that . . .
. . . you couldn't bottle it up, even after a lousey day

Edward Vernon was an unpopular admiral who commanded the British fleet in the West Indies in the mid-18th century. He was well known for wearing a coat made from a mixture of silk, mohair and gum called 'grogram', which earned him the nickname Old Grog. At one point he ordered that the twice daily issue of neat rum served to his crew should be diluted, with a pint of water to a quarter of a pint of rum. This inevitably made him even less popular with his crew, and before long he was recalled to Britain. The weaker and less desirable alcoholic drink gained the name of GROG – though the word is now used of undiluted alcoholic drinks as well. Grog, by the way, was still issued to sailors as late as 1970!

When the alcohol rations were issued at certain points in the day, some sailors would try to save theirs in a bottle and hide it away until night-time, so that they could then drink a whole day's rations in one go and get drunk. This could lead to fighting in the evening, and so it was against the rules to BOTTLE IT UP. If someone did bottle up his rations and then drink the lot in one go and fall asleep (or pass out), when he came round he would be described as feeling GROGGY.

The old English word *mes* meant a 'dish', and in particular a communal dish from which comrades would eat. Thus the officers' canteen on a ship came to be called the OFFICERS' MESS.

It was important that hammocks were rolled up tightly every day so that if there was a battle they did not take up unnecessary space. Every hammock had to be passed through a standard-size metal ring before it was stowed away to prove it had been rolled properly. From this idea came a phrase associated with passing a test. It has evolved over time into the idea of a person's body going through a ring like a hammock, to mean having to meet various criteria: PASSING THROUGH THE HOOPS or JUMPING THROUGH HOOPS.

Head lice were very common in the cramped and generally insanitary conditions on board a galleon. If you discovered that you had the little parasites, you would say that it had been a LOUSEY DAY – or 'lousy day' as we now spell it. Sailors used to wear their hair long, tied in a pony-tail at the back of their head. To keep this in place and to discourage lice they would dip it in tar. Hence they were called TARS. The common version of the name John was often applied generically by aristocrats to commoners whose names it was not worth remembering. This certainly applied to sailors, and hence the generic name for a sailor came to be JACK TAR. (By the same principle, a man who worked high up on churches was called a STEEPLEJACK and a tree feller a LUMBERJACK.) Before the 20th century and the use of steam-powered machinery on board fighting ships, manpower was in constant demand. Sailing a ship and firing the guns were very manually intensive (for example, *Victory* herself had a standard crew of 850 in a ship only 200 feet long). Everyone on board was expected to do whatever was needed – so, for example, marines would help push the capstan to raise the anchor, sailors would scrub the deck and sew sails and mend ropes. Hence the expression for someone who is multiskilled and capable of doing many different things: JACK OF ALL TRADES.

Sailors were always working with rope and needed their own knives, but they had to be sure the blades would be safe while they were moving about the rigging. Hence they developed a knife with a hinged blade that could be folded safely away into the handle. The name of this knife has been used in more modern times to describe the motion when an articulated lorry gets out of control by likening it to the motion of the blade when it is closing: JACK-KNIFE.

Soldiers were often collectively referred to by the weapons they used, such as bayonets or rifles: for example, one might talk about 'a hundred rifles'. In the same way, as sailors were constantly working with ropes they were referred to collectively as HANDS.

Four hundred years ago a word for a man in charge of something was 'swain'. So the man in charge of a ship's boat was called the BOATSWAIN or BO'SUN. The boat that the captain used would usually be stored on top of the main deck and, using the old word 'cock' meaning 'sticking up', this boat was called the COCKBOAT. The person in charge of this would be called a COCKSWAIN or COXSWAIN. This has now been shortened even further, so that the person who steers a rowing boat is called a COX.

Well, I never knew that . . .
. . . if you wanted food piping hot, you wouldn't loaf around

The bo'sun took orders from an officer and communicated them to the crew using a special whistle. These whistles gave

a piercing sound that could be heard even in battle and bad weather. In fact the correct name for it – the bo'sun's 'call' – comes from its purpose of calling for the attention of the crew. Each instruction would have its own series of notes, called a 'pipe'. For example, if an important person such as the captain or admiral came on board they would be PIPED ON BOARD. Also, mealtimes would be announced with a particular 'pipe'. Those crew members who would get to the mess tables first would get the food while it was still hot from the stove – PIPING HOT. Another command was to order sailors to go below decks, douse the lights and stop talking: hence the phrase PIPE DOWN. (Once 'pipe down' had been sounded, the actual ringing of the bells to mark the stages of each watch was stopped until the next morning.)

Despite all the efforts of ships' cats, the storage holds of galleons would often be infested with rats. If the ship were to sink these would scuttle to the surface and be seen clinging onto anything that floated. This gave the impression that they too were abandoning ship, giving rise to the expression LIKE RATS DESERTING A SINKING SHIP. (It then became legend that if a rat was seen to be leaving ship in port it was because the rat knew the ship was going to sink.) This tendency to resort to self-interest under duress also led to the phrase used of someone who switched loyalty and passed on confidential information, TO RAT ON SOMEONE. By analogy with a pig, there is a similar expression TO SQUEAL.

In 1753 a medical paper was presented to the Admiralty showing that lemon juice could prevent scurvy, a serious illness caused by lack of vitamin C that was common among sailors on long voyages, who had little or no fresh food while at sea. Initially lemons were purchased from the Mediterranean, but it was then discovered that lime juice could also be used. One of the senior admirals owned a lime plantation in the Caribbean and before long it was limes that were used primarily throughout the British navy to prevent crews getting scurvy. Other countries did not immediately copy the British, and so British ships and their crews became known as LIMEYS – an expression still used by Americans for British people today.

Personal equipment for the crew was very basic on these ships. Plates were made simply by taking a plank of wood and cutting off a section, so that the sailor would have a SQUARE MEAL. (The squares made for easier stacking and more efficient storage.) Small pieces of wood called 'fiddles' would be nailed around the edges of these plates to stop the food slopping off onto the decks. Often a sailor would cheat by making his bigger so that he could take more food than the

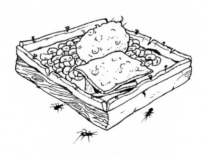

others. He would be ON THE FIDDLE. Bread would typically be collected from the bakery by one sailor for everyone on his mess table. The bakery would be a warm room, and in cold weather the messenger might be tempted to hang around there. Hence an expression developed meaning taking one's time: LOAFING AROUND – or, as they still say in the navy, GOING FOR LOAF – meaning bunking off.

Galleons would set sail with barrels full of salted meat which would be used up through the voyage. When a barrel was empty of meat there would still often be remnants of fat at the bottom which would then be used in cooking. Hence SCRAPING THE BOTTOM OF THE BARREL.

When meat was boiled, the grease that rose to the surface was called 'slush'. This was skimmed off and used to waterproof rope. The cook would keep some for himself, which he sold to other sailors to waterproof their clothes. The money he received as a result of this private trading was called a SLUSH FUND.

French adventurers who used Caribbean islands as bases or repair grounds became used to the local style of cooking food on frames called 'boucans' which were held over open fires. This gave rise to a nickname for such pirates: 'BOUCANEERS' OR BUCCANEERS.

There were many protocols to be observed on board ship. For example, if an officer was wearing a hat he had to be saluted, and it was considered insubordination not to do so. If he was holding his hat, however, he did not need to be saluted. An officer had to wear his jacket on deck and could remove it only when he retired below decks to the room where officers ate their meals. Here there would be a wardrobe where they could hang their coats. Hence the officers' mess on board a ship was called the WARDROOM. The captain of a ship traditionally eats alone and can enter the wardroom only at the request of his officers.

A device was developed in the French navy for situations where the crew had a dispute with an officer but where no one person was prepared to act as leader or spokesman for fear of punishment. The people involved would get a ribbon (*ruban* in French) or some other piece of parchment or cloth and join the ends so that it formed a continuous loop. They would then all sign it and deliver it to the captain so that it contained everyone's name, but without any one name being at the top of a list. The stratagem was adopted in the British navy, using a round piece of cloth or paper which the crew signed around the edge – again avoiding any one name appearing at the top of a list. The French name for this device, *rond ruban*, mutated into the English term ROUND ROBIN – though it is now more commonly used for any letter sent to many people.

Well, I never knew that . . .
. . . when there was enough room to swing a cat, the holy trinity
would leave its mark

Soldiers on board ship, as opposed to the sailors who manned the vessels, were named after the Latin word for sea, MARINES.

These soldiers were used not just to kill enemies but also to control the crew, many of whom would have been convicted criminals or in the navy against their will, having been press-ganged. Discipline was very severe.

A particularly grim punishment was to be hung over the side of the ship by your hands tied together, and then have another rope tied to your feet and run under the ship and up the other side. This latter rope would then be pulled, dragging you down one side of the hull, under the ship and up the other side. Not only was there clearly a danger of drowning in the process, but the bottoms of these ships attracted razor-sharp barnacles and other crustaceans, so that your body, arms, legs and face would be lacerated as you went – all of course in salt water – ouch! No wonder a double dose of this punishment was considered equivalent to a death sentence. As the person being punished would have to be hauled over the keel at the bottom of the hull, the ordeal was called KEEL HAULING – a term now used to describe a very severe punishment that in career terms is potentially fatal.

When Swedish sailors were punished they would be made to run, naked, down a 'corridor' formed by two ranks of sailors, who would beat them with knotted rope as they went. This punishment, whose name came from two words, *gata*, meaning a way or passage, and *lopp*, meaning a course, was adopted by other countries, and in England by the Royal Navy, where the unfamiliar Swedish words mutated into a similar-sounding English term. Thus the practice became known as making someone RUN THE GAUNTLET.

Probably the most common punishment was flogging. Whips were made of several strands of rope or leather, often with a small piece of metal tied into the tip of each strand to cause even worse wounds. The wounds caused by these whips were similar to deep claw marks and so the whips were called CATS. Some cats had three tails, representing the Trinity of God the

Father, the Son and the Holy Ghost. When used on land, this instrument was sometimes referred to as a 'scourge'. However, it was considered far more efficacious in terms of both religion and punishment to have an even more holy *trinity of trinities* – hence the more usual naval whip, the CAT O' NINE TAILS.

In the days of the sailing ships, life below decks was very cramped. Even though men of the 18th century were on average about 4 inches shorter than we are today, they could not stand up straight below decks. Therefore if there was a punishment whipping it had to take place up on the open deck because down below there was NOT ENOUGH ROOM TO SWING A CAT. The cat was always stored in a bag of a particular colour – red, to hide the bloodstains. If a crime on board a ship was discovered and it was likely that it would result in a flogging, the sailors would say 'THE CAT IS OUT OF THE BAG'. After a flogging, salt would usually be put on to the wounds. Clearly this would be excruciatingly painful and therefore continue the punishment. It also acted as an antiseptic and meant the wounds would heal more quickly, enabling the sailor to return to full duties as soon as possible. From this practice we get the phrases RUBBING SALT INTO THE WOUND, making a bad situation worse, and 'DON'T RUB IT IN', meaning things are bad enough without any more aggravation; also 'THERE'S THE RUB', referring to a further disadvantage of a course of action. Incidentally, sailors had to pay for the salt used to treat these wounds. So there was a double whammy after a flogging: not only the pain of the salt, but also the pain of having to pay for it!

For a ceremonial flogging where the whole crew would be forced to watch, the sailor would be manacled to a vertical board to hold him still while being flogged. On other occasions, he might simply be tied in position lying on top of a barrel. Hence when someone is helpless and at someone else's mercy, we say they have him OVER A BARREL. For very serious offences, where an example was to be made to deter any other sailor from repeating the crime, the sailor would be flogged in turn in front of the crew of every ship in the fleet – FLOGGED AROUND THE FLEET. This was essentially a very painful death sentence.

Some captains were particularly fond of using the cat to keep discipline and during a journey of several months or even years would preside over many floggings. In these cases the person giving the flogging on one occasion might be concerned that he would suffer the same fate next time around. This might make him hold back the full force of the whip, and also refrain from the technique of whipping his hand back at the last moment to accelerate the ends of the whip so that they would lacerate the victim's back as much as possible. This holding back was known as 'scratching', although in practice this would still cause very bloody and painful cuts; the deal among the sailors was 'I'LL SCRATCH YOUR BACK IF YOU SCRATCH MINE.'

Sometimes the victim of a flogging would die. In some cases this was actually intended, but often it was not and would be seen as a pointless and ultimately unproductive exercise of the kind we mean when we talk of FLOGGING SOMETHING TO DEATH.

Incidentally, use of the 'cat' has never been abolished in the Royal Navy, only suspended!

Another treatment for flogged sailors – and a common treatment for injuries and diseases of all sorts – was the application of vinegar as an antiseptic, along with brown paper laid over the area to reduce bleeding. So common was it, in fact, that it appears in a well-known nursery rhyme – although the childish verses are not quite what they seem! At this time 'tumbling down' was a euphemism for sex, and 'breaking a head' (or sometimes crown) was a euphemism for losing one's virginity. 'Head' was also used as a nickname for the male member (and still is in some phrases). Hence the real meaning of the rhyme is to tell how a boy has a liaison with a more experienced girl, loses his virginity, catches a venereal disease, and then needs to get treatment from the local crone. The girl, meanwhile, returns home, pleased with her conquest, only to be chastised by Jack's mother . . .

Jack and Jill went up the hill,
To fetch a pail of water
Jack fell down and broke his crown
And Jill came tumbling after.

Up Jack got and home did trot
As fast as he could caper,
To old dame dob who patched his nob,
With vinegar and brown paper.

When Jill came back, she did grin
To hear of Jack's paper plaster.
So his mother whipped her across her knee
For causing Jack's disaster.

The third line of the second verse has changed over time to disguise the sexual nature of the poem and is often given as *'he went to bed to mend his head'* – although even here the reference to his 'head' is kept. Given how unlikely it is that anyone would fetch water from *up* a hill, it shows that the pair's naïve attempt to disguise their liaison was very transparent.

In 1789, the crew of a ship off the coast of Tahiti had to decide between sailing all the way back to Britain under the harsh and cruel regime of a tyrannical captain to deliver their cargo of fruit or to stay in the tropical island paradise and settle in with the beautiful local girls. Understandably they chose the latter, and so they marooned the captain and his officers in a boat in the middle of the ocean. The crew then successfully hid on the volcanic Pitcairn Islands for over 20 years before being discovered. In fact, the descendants of these original mutineers and the wives they took with them from Tahiti still live on the island – although the population is often no more than 50 individuals. Incredibly, the captain survived 3,500 miles at sea to make landfall in Java. The incident came to be known as THE MUTINY ON THE *BOUNTY*, after Captain Bligh's ship.

Well, I never knew that . . .
. . . snotties and reefers might hail from good families who couldn't make ends meet

The younger sons of country gentry would sometimes choose, or be sent by their families, to become trainee naval officers. These boys – often not even teenagers – would be stationed in the middle of the ship's deck when on duty so that they could quickly get to anywhere they were needed. As a result they were called MIDSHIPMEN. Clearly, youngsters standing out in the elements would often have had runny noses – hence

their nickname SNOTTIES. To discourage them from wiping their noses on their arms, the uniform had buttons sewn on the lower sleeves. One of the duties of midshipmen was to supervise the 'reefing in' of the topsails, and so they were also known as REEFERS. They could not carry out this task in the full long-tailed coats usually worn by officers as these would have been too cumbersome aloft. Instead, they wore a short, heavy woollen coat that gave them more flexibility. This style of coat subsequently became known as a REEFER JACKET. (Incidentally, the resemblance of self-rolled marijuana cigarettes to furled topsails has also given rise to the street name REEFERS.)

Trading ships encountering each other at sea would often sail close and hail each other, asking where the other came from and whether there was any news from that port. Hence the expression TO HAIL FROM somewhere, meaning to come from a place.

When the triangular 'jib sails' at the front of ships were adopted by European navies, different nations used different variants. This enabled lookouts to identify at least the nationality of a ship at a great distance. The captain could then assess whether an approaching vessel was likely to be hostile and decide what course of action was appropriate. By analogy, naval officers who had come to an instant view about someone simply by their dress and appearance would say: 'I DON'T LIKE THE CUT OF YOUR JIB.'

Galleons had an enormous amount of rigging to hold the masts in place, to allow crew to climb up the masts and to control the sails. On HMS *Victory* there were 26 miles of ropes in the rigging! These ropes quickly frayed and needed running repairs, especially at the ends. Whenever there was little else to do the crew would be set to work on mending these ropes, to keep them busy and so avoid unrest, fighting and the risk of mutiny. Thus having nothing of importance to do was called BEING AT A LOOSE END, and sorting out details that were not sufficiently important to demand attention when there were other priorities came to be known as TIDYING UP LOOSE ENDS. Repairing these ropes often involved twisting or even spinning the cords to make strong rope, and while doing this the sailors would tell each other stories, a habit which became known as SPINNING A YARN.

Small, useless bits of rope were known by a word that we still use today to describe old things that you have never got around to throwing away: JUNK. Sailors would gather these small bits together, unpick them and then sell them to shipyards for use in caulking (making waterproof) the planking on decks or making paper boards. This was an easy (though illegal) way of making money – MONEY FOR OLD ROPE.

After a battle the crew would often be able to improvise a repair to a damaged rope, even if it had been shot through, by splicing in other, shorter pieces of rope left over from something else. From this we get a phrase associated nowadays with scrimping and saving, MAKING ENDS MEET.

Ropes often need to be repaired or joined together using a method called 'splicing'. This process involves unwinding the ends of two ropes and then rewinding them together so they are interwoven. This has given us a phrase originally used when a sailor was married: GETTING SPLICED. One of the most important ropes on a galleon was the rope (or 'brace') that held the main mast in place. This rope was very thick and kept very tight to withstand the enormous pressures of the wind blowing on the sails. Occasionally, usually after a battle, it was necessary to replace this rope. Because this was a difficult and heavy job, which required the whole crew pulling to create the necessary tension, a tradition developed in the Royal Navy that the crew would have an extra rum ration after completing it. Hence the phrase now used outside the navy as well to mean having a celebratory drink – SPLICE THE MAINBRACE. Another word for this rope has given us a phrase to describe someone or something at the heart of a team: the MAINSTAY.

When sailors had to haul ropes in they would pull first with a hand on one side, then with the other hand on the other side – hence the phrase HAND OVER FIST. Due to the frequency of this activity on board a ship the expression came to mean 'easy but effective', especially applied to making money.

During long voyages, repairs had to be made to wooden sailing ships while they were still at sea. One such task was to ensure that the seals between the planks round the waterline were all secure. The main seam in this part of the hull was known as the 'devil', and when sailors hung on ropes over the side to complete any running repairs they were said to be BETWEEN THE DEVIL AND THE DEEP BLUE SEA.

Peier is the Old French word meaning to brush with hot tar (from the Latin *picare*, to cover with pitch), from which we get the naval term 'to pay' with the same meaning. If a ship was in need of attention in this area and there was no tar with which to do it, there would be trouble ahead – hence a phrase meaning just that: THE DEVIL TO PAY AND NO HOT PITCH (often shortened to simply 'the devil to pay').

The French word meaning 'to sing' is *chanter*, from which we get the word for rhythmical songs sung by sailors, designed to help them all heave together on the beat when pulling on ropes or around the capstan: a SEA SHANTY.   **WINKT!**

3

Ships and Shipbuilding

As styles of fighting ship developed
over the centuries, so new skills and mechanisms
developed – and their names are still with us,
long after the galleons have gone.

Well, I never knew that . . .
. . . dogs and dragons both go back to the Vikings

Vikings were feared for their reputation of sailing to foreign lands with the aim of stealing gold and livestock, and abducting the natives into slavery. Not much was known about them except that they were believed to come from the north, and so they were called NORSEMEN. These raiders had clear objectives in terms of what they were after, but did not much mind where they got it – so they were called SEA ROVERS, derived from the word 'roving' used to describe travellers who wandered around the countryside looking for food and prepared to cause trouble to get it. These land-based travellers would often have half-trained dogs with them for company, and to intimidate peasants, and so a common nickname evolved for dogs that had a master: ROVER. A romanticized view of the Viking adventurers confidently exploring foreign lands and relishing the excitement of their travels led to a brand name for a 20th-century form of transport, ROVER cars. The Vikings had the head of a dragon on the front prow of their boats which gave

them the name DRAGON BOATS. A Viking dragon boat appears on the Rover car badge.

In Viking law, the eldest son inherited everything on the death of his father. So as the population grew and land became scarce, second and subsequent sons were forced to emigrate and invade areas of England and northern France, with the intention of settling there permanently. In north-western France this led to the Viking settlers being named NORMANS (a shortening of Norsemen) and the land they had acquired was called NORMANDY. In England King Alfred the Great had to buy off the Danish Vikings by paying them in gold to stop them fighting. This payment was called DANEGELD. He was also forced into a truce which resulted in the Vikings ruling the northern and eastern parts of England. In these areas

Danish law applied, and the area was known as the DANELAW. One part of this law stated that if someone failed to pay the Vikings' high taxes in full, he would be punished by mutilation of the nose; so now we call paying an excessive price PAYING THROUGH THE NOSE. This phrase was then amusingly adapted by a major petrol company for an advertising campaign designed to underpin their low pricing policy: DON'T PAY THROUGH THE NOZZLE! The Viking tax was an example of payment extracted by intimidation and extortion; even now we describe an unreasonably high price as EXTORTIONATE.

Viking boats were essentially designed for transporting invaders and their equipment, and for taking slaves and loot back home. Thus they had to be built to survive the ravages of the voyage across the wild North Sea, and were far larger than most boats of that period; so they were often called LONGBOATS. By the Middle Ages, naval vessels were increasingly being used to fight one another at sea. This led to warships having castle-like superstructures, with battlements built at both ends to provide fighting platforms for the soldiers on board. The rear of the ship was called the after or

aft' castle, and the front of the ship the forecastle or FO'C'SLE. Usually, the captain would have the rearmost cabin because the broad stern end of the ship allowed for a wider, more comfortable room with windows and better light. His officers' cabins would be next to his. Collectively, approximately one-fourth of the ship was allocated to the officers. Hence the deck above their rooms was called the QUARTERDECK, and the rooms themselves the OFFICERS' QUARTERS. The idea of referring to the officers' living area in this way then spread to the army, where it came to mean accommodation more generally. By the late 16th century the area where prisoners would be kept was called 'prisoners' quarters', and so, by extension, soldiers being instructed not to take prisoners in a battle would be told to 'GIVE NO QUARTER!' In other words, don't leave anyone alive who will need to be kept in the prisoners' quarters.

Viking boats were powered by both sail and oars, and steered by one great oar on the right-hand side of the boat at the back, controlled by the *steersmen*. Hence this side of the boat was known as the *steerboard* side or STARBOARD. The area towards the back of the boat where the steering took place was called the STERN. While Viking boats could be run up onto beaches, when they were brought into a port they would come in with the steerboard away from the quay to avoid damage and ensure maximum control. Hence the cargo was unloaded (*laded*) on the other side, which became known as the LADEBOARD or LARBOARD side. However, because of the similarity in sound, this word was often confused with 'starboard', and so over time it became known by a different name: the side which was tied up to the quay, hence the PORT side. A good way of remembering which is which is that whenever we drink port, some of the port is always *left* at the bottom of the glass. This also reminds us that the international maritime regulations require all ships to display at night a red light on the port side and a green light on the starboard side.

The old Viking word for the side of a boat is *borth*, related to Old English *bord*. If someone accidentally falls over it they are said to be OVERBOARD. When a mast was blown away in battle and fell over the side of the ship it would usually have to be cut free by hacking through the rigging so that it did not impair the movement of the ship. When this happened the mast was said to have GONE BY THE BOARD – meaning gone for good. In the days of galleons many fleet actions were decided by one or more ships banging into the enemy ships, enabling the crew to attack by swinging on ropes, climbing the rigging or leaping over the side of the ship – BOARDING. Immediately prior to such an assault, the boarding crew would be ordered to wherever contact was about to be made, often at the bows; hence the phrases AT THE SHARP END and LOOK SHARP!

Well, I never knew that . . .
. . . if you don't keep an even keel, you might be on
your beam ends

When a galleon was built, the first piece to be put in place would be the keel. Every other part of the ship would ultimately be connected back to this critical component, and so it would be placed in a carefully constructed wooden frame or 'bed'. Hence the phrase for beginning to construct a ship: TO LAY THE KEEL (in the bed). It was vital that this was level, otherwise the whole ship's construction would suffer. So, just as a ship must be BUILT ON AN EVEN KEEL, so someone who has reformed their bad behaviour or perilous financial situation is said to be BACK ON AN EVEN KEEL. The heavy horizontal timbers that support the deck and brace the two sides of the hull are called beam timbers, as they reach from one beam to the other. If the ship is heeling over so much that these timbers are nearly vertical the ship is clearly in real difficulty, just like someone in dire financial straits, who may be said to be ON HIS BEAM ENDS.

The places where ships were constructed became highly specialist areas where the space, equipment and manpower were all dedicated to this single task. Using the old English term for an area of land, a 'yard', we get the word SHIPYARD. The same goes for the area where ships would load and unload cargoes, named after the side of the port designed for ships to tie up to: the DOCKYARD. Even today we use a related word to describe a receiving device for a portable computer, phone, or any kind of hi-tech equipment designed to connect or load/unload data to or from the device: the DOCKING STATION.

Greek and Roman ships would typically have an area at the back of the ship dedicated to the god or goddess that was looking after the ship and crew. This would often include a statue or at least a bust of the head and shoulders of this patron deity. These statues were usually carved from wood, and from the Latin word *figura* meaning 'to shape' we get the word used to describe such models of humans, a 'figure'. Hence, military toys would be toy soldier FIGURES. This word is also used to describe the shape of humans; for example, an attractively shaped woman may be said to have A GOOD FIGURE. (The word 'figure' meaning 'shape' also gives us the word used for the shape of the symbols used to depict numerical amounts, and hence the amounts themselves – FIGURES – and the idea of calculating a mathematical question: FIGURING IT OUT.)

These traditions continued and evolved until the age of the galleons from the 15th century onwards, when it was traditional to have a large carving of a person or mythical creature at the front of the hull to convey good luck and personality to the ship. As this figure was placed at the front or 'head' of the ship, it was called a FIGUREHEAD – not because

it was a head (it would usually be at least the head and torso). While this feature could be important in keeping up morale in the crew and providing the ship with an identity, clearly it could play no practical part in the functioning of the ship. So today we use the word for someone who is significant in representing an organization but doesn't take part in the actual work.

In early whaling ships massive logs of wood were embedded in the deck near the front of the ship, to which the ropes from the harpoons were attached. This log became the straining point of the battle between the whale and the ship which would end only when the whale was dead or the ship overturned. As these pieces of wood were always in the bows of the ships they were called LOGHEADS or LOGGERHEADS – a word now used to describe a conflict in which neither side will back down.

Planks of wood in the hull of a galleon were often nailed into place with quite a curve on them to provide a strong and streamlined shape. Sometimes these would spring loose, especially if the fixings had been weakened over time or in battle. This has given us a phrase used to describe a trickle of water that becomes a flow – or, more recently, urinating: to SPRING A LEAK.

The masts of the great galleons were massive: those of *Victory* stretched to over 300 feet high. At intervals up each mast there were mini-decks where rigging could be tied off and adjusted and from where snipers could fire in battles (Nelson was killed by a French sharpshooter in such a position). These mini-decks, called 'tops', were reminiscent of the distinctive birds' nests visible high up in trees in winter, and hence came to be known colloquially as CROWS' NESTS.

The long wooden cross-pieces on masts that hold up the sails are named after the Viking word for stick, *gyrd*, a word that found its way into English as YARD.

The Dutch have a long history of sea travel and have given us two words fundamentally associated with it. The first is their word for 'roof', which was initially used to describe a solid wooden structure that protected the crew and cargo from the weather, as well as providing a flat upper floor for the vessel. The word is *dec*, from which we get DECK.

Grapeshot was a particularly vicious version of cannon fire, consisting of many small balls the size of golf balls all fired at once – a missile that would scythe down anyone in its way. If officers anticipated an enemy was going to fire grapeshot, an order would be shouted so that the crew could dive for cover by lying down on the deck behind the protective gunwales: 'HIT THE DECK!'

During a fight on board a ship, if a man was knocked over with such force that he was unable to jump back up quickly, he was said to have been DECKED.

The raised wall of wood that went around the top deck was named using the Saxon words for tree (*bole*) and work (*woerc*): BULWARK. It was found very early in the history of shipbuilding that if the ship was to be stable these walls should be broadest below the waterline and then get narrower higher up. Hence the pear-shaped cross-section of early galleons. This roundness of the hull reminded the French of a bag that they called a *bougle*, from which we get the word BULGE. The bottom of the boat was also where any water that leaked into the ship would end up, and so the pumps to clear this water away were usually located slightly higher up, often at the height of the widest part of the bulge. Hence the pumps became known as 'bulge' or BILGE PUMPS. Another version of this phrase has subsequently become used to compare an idea or remark to the dirty and festering water at the bottom of a ship: BILGE WATER or simply BILGE.

Battens are sticks that are used like bolts to lock hatches in position. When a storm is coming the crew need to ensure that the rough seas will not enter the cargo area and so damage what they are carrying. Hence the instruction now used more widely of actions taken in anticipation of a tough time: 'BATTEN DOWN THE HATCHES.'

In emergencies such as storms or battles it was important to be able to release ropes quickly but without having to cut them. The most common form of quick release mechanism was a sturdy stick about 20 inches long that could be pushed into a hole. Rope would then be wound around it above and below the hole to secure it. When the stick was pulled out, the rope would instantly be released without having to be laboriously unwound. These sticks, resembling giant pins, were called BELAYING PINS. Their use to stop ropes from slipping led to the word being used in an analogous sense to mean 'holding' or cancelling an order: BELAY THAT ORDER!

When a galleon was tied up to a quay in port, the ropes and chains would be secured to heavy posts sunk into the deck called 'bits'. The parts of the ropes that went around these posts were often formed into loops called 'bitters' after the post. Hence the phrase TO THE BITTER END, meaning doing something all the way to the very end (both from the fact that the journey had come to an end and because the end of the rope was tied to the bit). The French word *jeter*, meaning 'to throw', is associated with anything that has been thrown over the side of a ship. Thus, to throw something over the side is to JETTISON it. The discarded item(s) then becomes referred to as JETSAM. The French word *flotter*, to float, is associated with bits of floating wreckage or FLOTSAM. Combine the two and we have FLOTSAM AND JETSAM.

Well, I never knew that . . .
. . . powder monkeys are more use than loose cannons

In the days of galleons, ships carried gunpowder below the waterline to reduce the risk of its being hit directly by an enemy cannonball and exploding. Even in the middle of a battle, only enough powder for a few shots was kept near each gun, and a constant supply of new charges was brought up from the magazines by a chain of men. It was the job of very young boys (some as young as ten) to run between the hatches on each deck and the guns, dodging the men and the firing cannons, to keep the guns supplied with powder. The incredible speed at which they performed this essential task earned them the nickname MONKEYS or POWDER MONKEYS.

Cannonballs were extremely heavy, and as very few were explosive (most were simply solid lumps of iron) they could be stored alongside the guns. But storing such large and round objects on a flat deck was not easy, and so a thick plank of wood with holes in was used to hold the balls in position ready for use. This too was called a MONKEY.

In the onshore batteries, these cannonball-holders were often made in a triangular shape, and were commonly made of brass so that they would last longer and not rust. Three or six holes were made to hold the first layer of balls, and then more balls were stacked on top in layers, forming a pyramid. However, in very cold weather the iron cannonballs would contract at a different rate from the brass plate, so that sometimes the balls would pop out of position and fall to the ground. Hence COLD ENOUGH TO FREEZE THE BALLS OFF A BRASS MONKEY.

In a storm everything that could move around had to be securely tied in place, and this was especially true of the big cannons which could cause mayhem and many deaths if allowed to roll around the deck in a rough sea. If a cannon did break free from its ropes sailors would call 'Loose cannon on the deck!' Nowadays we use the term to describe someone who is unpredictable and who could cause a great deal of harm through their wild actions: a LOOSE CANNON.

In the cramped conditions of a galleon it was vital that anything superfluous was cleared away before a battle to ensure it did not get in the way, and also to avoid its being hit by a cannonball and becoming a deadly missile itself. Hence the order 'CLEAR THE DECKS FOR ACTION!' – or, as is often said now, simply 'clear the decks'.

The Greek word *anklos* meaning 'to bend' gives us several words including the name for parts of our legs that bend, ANKLES, and the measure of the bend in a line, ANGLE. Related to this is the word to describe people who use a bent piece of metal on a line to catch fish: ANGLERS. Of more relevance here is the word used to describe a very large bent piece of metal that is used to keep a ship in position: ANCHOR.

The larger the vessel, the larger and heavier the anchor had to be if it was to secure the ship. Some anchors were massive: on Nelson's flagship HMS *Victory* the capstan used to haul up the anchors went through two decks and required 260 men to work it efficiently. The word used to describe this activity is derived from the Old Saxon word *woeg*, which meant 'to move or carry': to WEIGH ANCHOR. Incidentally, the same root has given us the word meaning to assess the mass of an object, TO WEIGH, and the phrase for a substantial problem, A WEIGHTY ISSUE.

The triangular points on the ends of an anchor are designed to catch in the sand or on rock. This process is by no means successful every time, and so their name has become associated with a lucky event – a FLUKE or FLUKEY.

When weighing anchor, the anchor rope would be hauled up on to the deck, where it would need to be secured or 'nipped' into place with short pieces of rope that could quickly be released when the anchor was dropped again. With many of the adult crew members needed to haul the anchor in, the task of securing the cable in this way was often left to young and nimble boys or NIPPERS. The word 'nip' then came to be used more widely with a general meaning of 'constrain'. In particular, it was used by horticulturalists to stop some buds from flowering so that the plant's energy would be focused on those buds that were left. This was done by cutting below the bud before it flowered. This phrase is now used metaphorically when an idea or suggestion is prevented from emerging fully – when it is NIPPED IN THE BUD.

Well, I never knew that . . .
. . . if you're told to sling your hook, it maybe time to cut and run

Once the anchor, colloquially called the 'hook' by sailors, has been weighed, it then needs to be secured in a sling against the side of the ship so it cannot swing free and damage the hull while in rough seas. Hence a phrase referring to a ship leaving port, nowadays used to tell someone to go away: 'SLING YOUR HOOK!'

Even when a ship is anchored, the winds, tides and currents continue to move it around, and so it is necessary to stay some way away from it to avoid being hit as it swings and shifts. The phrase used to reinforce this good advice is now used of anything that is to be avoided – GIVE IT A WIDE BERTH. Sometimes a ship was anchored at both ends to stop this swinging, a technique for which the Dutch used their word for 'retard', *marren*, from which we get our word MOORED.

On occasion – for example, if attacked without warning – ships needed to leave their moorings at very short notice.

With this in mind, the sails could be furled in such a way that only a few lines needed to be cut to allow them to drop into place and instantly catch the wind or RUN WITH THE WIND. Occasionally even the anchor rope would be cut to save the time taken to pull it on board. Thus a ship could CUT AND RUN.

Another way to save the time spent pulling up the anchor was simply to detach the anchor cable from the ship and let it slip out through the hole designed for it – to SLIP THE CABLE. This in turn gave rise to a phrase associated with escaping from an enemy ship or fleet bearing down on the port: to GIVE THEM THE SLIP.

When a small boat was coming alongside a larger boat in rough weather the waves coming back off the hull of the larger boat could make the sea even rougher, buffeting the smaller vessel. A technique sometimes used to lessen this effect and make it easier for the small boat to approach was to pour oil into the sea. This oil would quickly spread out and act as a 'skin' on top of the water, reducing the height of the waves and often stopping them from breaking. This gave rise to the phrase POURING OIL ON TROUBLED WATERS.

Well, I never knew that . . .
. . . if someone aims a broadside at you, you need to
pull your finger out

Having a deck running the full length of the vessel was a very important development, and this significance is acknowledged in the terminology that became established to distinguish different kinds of vessels. Strictly speaking, a *boat* is a vessel that does not have a continuous top deck, while one that does is called by a name derived from the Dutch *scip*: SHIP. The Dutch word *scip* originally meant simply a large vessel, which is why the Viking boats – correctly classified as such because they have no continuous upper deck – were originally called 'longships', because in those days the word was used more generally. This same Dutch word also gives us the name of a 20th-century receptacle for the disposal of rubbish, which resembles the shape of a boat: SKIP; and the word for the officer in charge of a ship: SKIPPER.

To build a ship – even a small boat – required the skills of many craftsmen, including various specialists such as carpenters and blacksmiths. And once built, of course, the vessel needed a crew with the specialist knowledge of how to sail her. Collectively, all these skilled men were called 'sailing craftsmen', and over time the boats themselves took on a similar name: SAILING CRAFT.

The vast majority of cannons on a ship of the line pointed out of the long sides of the vessel, with relatively few at the narrow ends. When a ship fired all of its side guns the

cannonade could be devastating: the *Victory*, for example, could fire over 2,500 pounds of iron cannonballs in one close-range broadside. This onslaught was described in a word we still use to mean a blistering verbal attack on someone: a BROADSIDE.

If a ship could fire its cannonballs through the stern of an enemy ship, the projectiles would travel all the way along the length of the vessel, killing crew members, upturning guns, and causing chaos, injury and mayhem as they went. The word used to describe this kind of attack came from the analogy with the agricultural process of ripping weeds out of a field through a sweeping motion of an iron tool: RAKING.

When a cannon fired there would often be some unexploded gunpowder left in the barrel. The barrel would already be very hot, and so to prevent air flowing through the touch-hole and into the barrel, and so igniting this powder, a gunner would cover the touch-hole with his finger, covered in a special leather finger-glove. However, this had to be removed before the next charge was rammed down, otherwise the

compression of the air could cause an explosion. In the middle of a battle everything was done at frenetic speed and, given the consequences of getting it wrong, there was a very clear order for the gunner who did not get the timing exactly right: 'PULL YOUR FINGER OUT!'

The Carron metal foundry in Glasgow – famous for making metal items ranging from massive industrial equipment to cookers – created a very short type of cannon used to fire very large cannonballs (often two at once at very short ranges, where the accuracy provided by long barrels was less important), or hundreds of smaller balls to clear enemy decks. These cannons were named after the site of the foundry and are known as CARRONADES.

From the days of the Battle of Agincourt the word 'cock' has been associated with something that sticks up. So, for example, a wide-brimmed hat that has its brim folded up in two or three places (bicorned or tricorned) was called a COCKED HAT. Nelson wore such a hat at the Battle of Trafalgar. At the time, in the very popular game of skittles, if you were left with three skittles still standing in a triangle the shape was likened to that of a tricorned hat and a phrase developed for victory in a game by a wide margin: KNOCKED INTO A COCKED HAT.

Muskets such as the one with which Nelson was shot were fired by first pulling the flint back and upwards until it clicked into place. This was called COCKING THE GUN. Pulling the trigger then caused a flint to spark and ignite a small amount of gunpowder in an indentation called a 'pan'. This flame then passed through a small hole and ignited the main charge of gunpowder that was in the barrel behind the bullet. If the flint had not been properly 'cocked' then the gun would not fire properly and was described as GOING OFF HALF COCKED, from which we get the phrase meaning an ill-prepared suggestion, A HALF-COCKED IDEA. Equally, if the powder was damp or the hole was dirty, then the powder in the pan might ignite but the main charge in the barrel would not, leading to a misfire. This disappointing effect was called a FLASH IN THE PAN. **WINKT!**

4

All at Sea

As an island nation, Britain has throughout
its history been inextricably linked to the sea.
Not surprisingly, many terms with a seafaring
origin are now part of everyday language.

Bill of Lading

400 yds of rope ✓
200 blocks ✓
800 cases-biscuits ✓
50 lengths-oak ✓
800 gals-rum ✓
150 tins-cat food ✓
40 charts ✓
500 gals of tar ✓

Lt. _____ _____
Purser

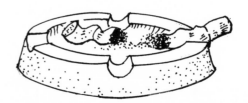

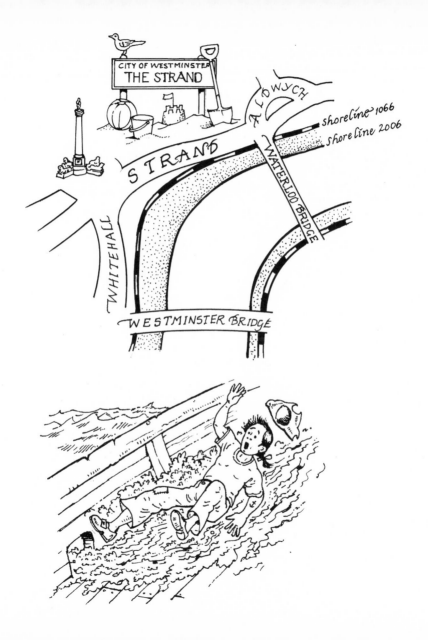

Well, I never knew that . . .

. . . if it doesn't 'fit the bill', it won't go 'down the hatch'

Landsmen who go to sea for the first time often feel unwell, feel scared due to the size of the ocean and lack confidence in the boat, having no idea what to do with the various ropes and sails etc. Hence the phrase meaning to be confused and worried about what to do: ALL AT SEA.

When a cargo was delivered and unloaded it would be checked off against the 'bill of lading', which was simply a list of everything that had been loaded at the start of the journey. If it was correct the people on the receiving end would say: 'THAT FITS THE BILL.'

Bill of Lading
400yds of rope ☑
200 blocks ☑
800 cases-biscuits ☑
50 lengths-oak ☑
800 gals-rum ☑
150 tins-cat food ☑
40 charts ☑
500 gals of tar
Lt. Unm Unmy
Purser

When goods are to be stored in the hold of a ship they are lowered through a hatch to the cargo area as rapidly as possible so that the ship can then set sail. By analogy, when someone has a drink, especially with a toast, and then swallows quickly they may well say: 'DOWN THE HATCH!'

The French word *escoutille*, meaning a hatchway, gave us a word meaning to cut a hole. This in turn was used to describe one way of sinking a ship from inside – by cutting a hole in the bottom of the hull. Hence our phrase TO SCUTTLE ONE'S OWN SHIP. When doing this, the last person involved in making the hole is going to be very quick in getting out, taking very rapid steps up the ladders – hence the phrase TO SCUTTLE ALONG. The same word can also be used to describe how an idea or plan is 'sunk' by other people's ideas or questions: to SCUTTLE AN IDEA.

Jactare is Latin for 'to throw'. Hence something that is thrown or forced *into* something is INJECTED. A part of a house or cliff that positively sticks out PROJECTS. The same Latin root also gives us the French word *jeter*, meaning 'to throw', and so a piece of a harbour that 'sticks out' into the sea is a JETTY.

Well, I never knew that . . .
. . . if you were up the pole you might well be scuppered

In storms, water would often crash onto the deck of a vessel. Special holes were made in the bulwarks of ships to let this water flow away. From the Old French word for 'to spit', *escopir*, we get the word for the holes: SCUPPERS. Now, the force of water coming through these holes could be very strong, and sailors could easily be knocked off their feet. Hence the phrase 'to be SCUPPERED'.

When a strong wind strikes a ship from the side, the vessel will be blown in the direction of the wind. It is therefore advisable for any other ship to leave considerable room on this side. The movement caused by the wind and subsequently the gap that should be left are both called by the same term we now use to describe the space we give someone to avoid problems: LEEWAY.

Even when a ship is anchored, it can still swing and move around in the tide and wind; so, when ships are being anchored in a harbour, even at specific berths, it is advisable to leave large gaps between them. Hence the phrase that refers to staying away from potential danger: to LEAVE A WIDE BERTH.

From the Viking word *strom*, meaning 'to flow', we get our word for a small river, STREAM. The same word gives us our names for a flag-like piece of material that 'flows' in the air, a STREAMER, and also the shape of something that flows easily through air or water: STREAMLINED. And we use a variant of the same word to describe a violent 'flowing' of wind and rain:

STORM. Combined with the Viking word *mael*, which means 'whirling around', this gives us the word for an extremely violent, swirling storm: MAELSTROM.

Sailors were expected to work the sails in all weathers. In storms, this involved climbing up the masts and rigging and moving along the yardarms high above the deck and the raging seas. In these conditions even the most experienced sailors could lose their grip and fall to their deaths. Hence such activity was considered madness by landlubbers and new recruits – but they would still be forced to do it. Using the slang word for a mast, pole, we get the expression for being sent mad, to be DRIVEN UP THE POLE, and the expression we use when someone has a daft idea: 'YOU'RE UP THE POLE'.

Well, I never knew that . . .
. . . if you keel over you might end up stranded in London

The bottom of Africa was originally named Cape of Storms by Bartholomew Diaz after the consistently bad weather he had encountered there. However, King John II of Portugal, wanting to encourage exploration and colonization in the east, renamed it the CAPE OF GOOD HOPE. This was a very significant point on the journey home for European sailors returning from voyages to the east, as the seas here were very dangerous, and once they were past it they could feel safer as they turned north towards home. From this we get the expression to have TURNED THE CORNER.

The Greek word for a ship was *naus*. This gives us the word for anything to do with ships, NAUTICAL, the name of the submarine in Jules Verne's story *Twenty Thousand Leagues under the Sea*, the NAUTILUS, and the feeling of sickness often experienced on board a ship, NAUSEA.

If a ship is in such strong winds that it heels over and exposes its keel it may well go all the way over. This gives us an expression used to describe when a person falls or collapses. We say they have KEELED OVER.

The ship's helmsmen played a very important role, and so they would be changed on a regular basis through a watch to ensure they were always fresh and alert. As these short spells on duty were considered a neat stunt to have pulled off, they were called TRICKS. By analogy, as the ladies of the night back in port would have several changes through the night, their customers were also called TRICKS.

The side of the ship that was facing the worst of a storm was called the weather side. Hence the phrase for someone who is successfully taking the brunt of major difficulties: WEATHERING THE STORM. The very worst conditions would be under the bow on the weather side of the ship, where the combination of the bad weather and the bow wave would make conditions very rough. Hence the phrase for not feeling too good: UNDER THE WEATHER BOW – often shortened to just UNDER THE WEATHER. Over time all sailors get used to spotting subtle signs that suggest a change of weather. Landlubbers looking at the same sky could not 'see' the signs, and so they would say that the experienced sailors had a WEATHER EYE. This phrase is now used for anyone in any specialist area who has the experience to spot early signs and trends that others cannot detect.

At the time of the Norman invasion of England in 1066, the word for a beach or shoreline was 'strand'. Hence the name of the road in central London that used to be the line of the beach of the Thames before the river bank was fixed in its current postion: THE STRAND. The word also gives us the word for the plight of a ship wrecked upon a beach or shoreline – and by extension the word for anyone who is left in a

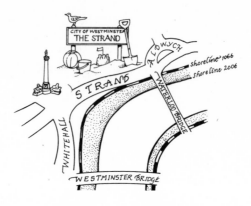

precarious situation: STRANDED. In fact it was only in Queen Victoria's reign that the current Thames shoreline was established as part of the land reclamation scheme. The land reclaimed on the north bank was named after her: THE VICTORIA EMBANKMENT.

Well, I never knew that . . .

. . . if you can't measure the sea, you can at least embrace it

When a channel or port has limited access, a ship must take a particular route to make way safely. The word for this is the same as that used for the 'safe' route to the green in golf: the FAIRWAY.

Faethm was an Old English word meaning 'to embrace'. The idea of someone extending their arms to the sides to give someone a hug gave rise to the word being used to name the measurement that was defined by the distance between two outstretched hands, approximately 6 feet: a FATHOM. By further analogy with a deep ocean measured in fathoms, the word became associated with deep thinking about unknown things: to FATHOM SOMETHING OUT.

Latitudo is the Latin word meaning 'breadth'. This gives us the word for the lines that go around the breadth of the globe, by which we measure positions from north to south on its surface: LATITUDE. We also use it to indicate the range or breadth within which someone must operate: if we allow them a lot of scope we say we are giving them a lot of LATITUDE.

The combination of storms, strong sunlight and constant use would gradually wear out sails and ropes. A shortened version of the word 'fatigued' became used to describe something that is getting tired or worn out. This was originally applied

to a worn-out edge of a piece of sailcloth or to a frayed piece of rope – the FAG END. Later it came to be applied to a used-up cigarette – FAG END – and also to the young boys in public schools who became tired running errands for older boys: FAGS. It also gives us the expression for someone who is exhausted: FAGGED OUT.   **WINKT!**

5

Navigation under Sail

In the days of the galleons, wind and
weather ruled – so no wonder we can hardly open
our mouths without referring to them,
even today.

Well, I never knew that . . .
. . . it took 16 bells to say 'Happy New Year'

If you are sailing directly towards another boat (i.e. with your bearing set directly at them) with the wind behind you it can be a threatening and intimidating approach. Hence the expression BEARING DOWN ON SOMEONE.

It was important at sea to spot other ships early. In order that the lookouts on a galleon were always fresh and alert, they would be changed every four hours. Hence the system of WATCHES. First watch, from 8 a.m. to 12 noon, was called the forenoon watch; the second, from noon to 4 p.m., was called the afternoon watch; and so on through the day and night. To make sure that everyone knew how far through the watch they were, the ship's bell was rung every 30 minutes. The first 30 minutes into a watch it was rung once; after another 30 minutes it was rung twice; and so on up to a sequence of eight rings to signify the end of the four-hour watch. Hence the phrase for the end of a watch: EIGHT BELLS. From this practice we also get an expression for a violent attack on someone that

stops just short of killing them – in other words, going to the stage just before the final one: BEATING SEVEN BELLS OUT OF SOMEONE.

There was a tradition whereby on New Year's Eve the youngest member of the crew rang the eight bells of the last watch as usual and then rang another eight bells to welcome the new year in: so he would RING OUT THE OLD AND RING IN THE NEW.

The watch between 4 p.m. and 8 p.m. was split into two parts of just two hours each. Because these watches were short and came towards the end of the day when the ship was beginning to relax, and included tea and dinner, they were named after the phrase the Romans used to refer to the lazy, hot midsummer days, 'the dog days': DOG WATCHES.

In 1797 a mutiny was planned to start when five bells were rung at 6.30 p.m. in the second 'dog watch'. However, the plot was uncovered and the officers rang the bell only once to fool the mutineers. This time is still rung with only one bell instead of five in the British Navy; and the following half-hours are rung with two bells, then three bells, then eight bells to signify the end of the dog watches and the start of the next watch.

Well, I never knew that . . .
. . . a safe harbour is the place for a good drink

The Latin word for a harbour or safe haven was *portus*. When ships were approaching a port with the wind against them they would often have to anchor out at sea until the weather changed. When the wind direction did change towards (Latin *ob*) the harbour, they would have the chance to move towards the port and then enter it or 'become one' with it – their ob-port-unity or OPPORTUNITY.

The idea of a ship carrying goods towards a port gave the French the word *porter*, meaning 'to carry', and hence our word for someone who carries things, a PORTER. We also have several related words, among them:

carryable – PORTABLE
carry away – DEPORT
carry into a country – IMPORT
carry out of a country – EXPORT
carry across some distance – TRANSPORT (*trans* means across)
carryable across some distance – TRANSPORTABLE

The Latin word *portus* also gives us another two words: the one we use for any harbour, PORT, and the name of a Portuguese city that was considered a very safe haven, despite the strong Atlantic gales around it: PORTO. In turn, the latter has given us the name for a fortified local wine: PORT. In fact, only wines made in this area can be called 'port'.

From an old Germanic word *flagga* meaning 'to falter' we get the word that describes how someone slows down when they are becoming very tired: to FLAG. By analogy with the way a piece of material blowing in the wind occasionally falls still, we get the same word applied to a banner or FLAG. In the Royal Navy, very senior officers would indicate their presence on a ship by flying a special flag. This enabled other ships and shore fortifications to see they were coming and issue an appropriate salute, such as firing a gun. Admirals would typically use a cross of St George with one or more large red dots marked on it indicating their rank: a rear admiral would show two dots, a vice admiral one dot, and a full admiral no dots at all. An admiral would typically choose to be based upon the biggest and best ship in the fleet, and hence these ships became known as FLAGSHIPS. This is why the best stores in a retail chain today are called FLAGSHIP STORES. At the Battle of Trafalgar HMS *Victory*, flying Nelson's flag, was a flagship of the Royal Navy in both senses. It remains one today: the oldest commissioned fighting ship in the world, still presided over by an admiral. His flag can still be seen flying on the *Victory* when he is present.

The idea of using coloured flags to send messages between ships gives us the phrase for pointing out something: to FLAG it.

The flag a ship carries clearly displays its nationality, and generates enormous pride and loyalty. It is the colours and designs on the flag that distinguish it, and hence at sea these flags are called COLOURS. Not surprisingly, a ship returning to its home port after a successful voyage will proudly display its flags for all to see, coming in WITH FLYING COLOURS. If a ship was captured, the victors would immediately replace the original flag with their own; accordingly, an internationally agreed custom became established that if a ship wished to surrender it would bring down its own flag or LOWER ITS COLOURS.

'Strike' is an old word meaning to hit someone hard, often with the consequence of knocking or bringing them down. Hence the word also came to be used in the sense of bringing things down, as in the phrase TO STRIKE ONE'S COLOURS or, in the army, when moving on every day, to STRIKE CAMP. If a ship was being chased by an attacker, another convention dictated that if the boat being pursued lowered its topsail to an unusually low level this indicated that it would slow down and surrender, and so the attacker should not keep firing at it as it caught up. Hence the less well-known phrase TO STRIKE ONE'S SAILS.

If a ship was already badly damaged but determined not to surrender under any circumstances, to avoid the danger of the flag being accidentally blown away the crew would NAIL ITS COLOURS TO THE MAST – a phrase that has come to be used to mean making an unequivocal statement of position or of support.

Pirates looking for treasure ships would often pretend to be from the same country as their quarry, putting up fake flags in order to lull the treasure ships into a false sense of security. Then at the last minute they would replace the dummy flag with their real pirate flag and attack. From this ruse we get the phrase SAILING UNDER FALSE COLOURS, meaning deliberately deceiving others as to your identity or purpose, and SHOWING YOUR TRUE COLOURS or SEEING SOMEONE IN THEIR TRUE COLOURS, meaning that their true intention or identity comes to light.

Navigators can assess their position in two ways. One is by looking at the stars and the sun, and the other is to calculate it by knowing where they were and then using course, speed, currents and wind to deduce where they are now. This 'deduced reckoning' was considered more accurate, and as the word 'dead' also meant 'exact' a new phrase developed: DEAD RECKONING.

The Greek word for stars, *astros*, has given us the name of people who journey towards the stars, ASTRONAUTS, and the way of forecasting the future through the stars, ASTROLOGY.

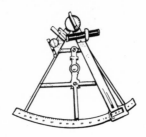

The science of studying the stars is called ASTRONOMY. When the Greeks blamed a bad event upon bad stars they used the negative prefix *dis* with *astros*, giving us DISASTROUS. An early navigational device that relied upon stars was called an ASTROLABE. A later device relied upon the sun and consisted of a device that could rotate along one-sixth of a circle; its name, deriving from the Latin word for 'six', was a SEXTANT. On the same basis, an earlier version that used only one-eighth of a circle was called an OCTANT.

Well, I never knew that . . .
. . . spelling is never plain sailing

The old name for a flat surface has also given its name to the tool that is used to make flat surfaces in carpentry, a PLANE. While navigators have known for centuries that the world is almost a sphere, for short distances it can be considered a flat surface for basic navigational calculations. This simplified form of navigational calculation has given rise to the phrase PLANE SAILING – now more usually, though in fact erroneously, spelt 'plain sailing'.

In former times the speed of a ship would be measured by throwing over the stern a specially shaped piece of wood (called a 'log') attached to a rope with knots in it at regular intervals. Depending upon how much rope was paid out in a given period of time, as measured by the sandglass, the ship's speed would then be recorded as a number of KNOTS. The speed in knots, direction, weather conditions, etc. would be written down every day in an official book that provided an entire record of the ship's voyage. The speed was one of the most important elements of this record, and so this book was called the LOG BOOK – a document with which we are now more familiar as the record of a car's history. If anyone needed to be punished on board ship, the crime and the punishment would also be recorded in the book – hence the expression TO BE LOGGED.

In shallow water, where there was a real risk of running aground, it was vital that the captain knew how deep the water was in front of the ship. So he would get a sailor to climb on to the bowsprit and drop a weighted line with knots at intervals into the water below. He would then shout out how many fathoms (the space between two knots was one fathom) deep the water was. From this practice we get two phrases with several meanings. From the use of the lead-weighted rope we get a phrase used nowadays to describe a *deeply* bad situation, often with tasteless behaviour: PLUMBING THE DEPTHS (from the Latin *plumbus*, meaning lead, referring

to the lead weight). The job of lying in the ropes by the bowsprit and occasionally throwing in a weighted line was seen as an easy job by other sailors and so a phrase has developed meaning malingering or taking the opportunity to have an easy time: SWINGING THE LEAD.

Sometimes the ocean floor would dip down or descend into a trench. In such circumstances the lead would not always have time to reach the bottom of the sea by the time the ship moved on. At least the ship was safe from grounding, but the crew did not know the depth of the water. This conundrum led to the phrase CANNOT FATHOM IT.

The area of sea that can be seen from (or off) the land used to be known as the offing. When a ship returning to port was first visible, it would be said to be IN THE OFFING, meaning its arrival was imminent. In the same way, when bad weather loomed, sailors would say, 'There's A STORM IN THE OFFING.' When a harbour had a tricky entrance, perhaps through rocks, shallows or dangerous currents, lights would be set up at night to guide ships in. The first light in this sequence leading to a safe berth was called the LEADING LIGHT – a phrase now meaning the most important or prominent thing or person in a group.

When a ship left a port it took with it a document (a bill) authorized by the port authorities, documenting that when it left neither it nor the port had any infectious diseases. So it was considered clean (not 'foul') and had been granted A CLEAN BILL OF HEALTH. If a ship did not have a clean bill of health on approaching a port it would be forced to wait offshore for 40 (in Latin, *quaranta*) days, after which, assuming there was still no illness on board, it would then be considered clean and be allowed into the port. The waiting period was called QUARANTINE.

Sailors' lives are dominated by the weather and so they will always be on the lookout for any changes – hence the phrase TO KEEP A WEATHER EYE ON SOMETHING, meaning to watch something continuously to pick up on the slightest change.

Well, I never knew that . . .

. . . a careful captain might keep his ship aloof

Whistling in the middle of a storm may seem a pointless and harmless thing to do as the wind will simply blow the sound away – hence the phrase TO WHISTLE IN THE WIND, meaning to do something futile. However, sailors have always been very superstitious, and in worsening weather whistling, which was associated with the sound of the wind in the rigging, was considered very bad luck, likely to attract an even worse storm. This was called WHISTLING UP THE WIND. Whistling under these conditions would therefore get a scared and very aggressive response from fellow sailors. Thus PUTTING THE WIND UP SOMEONE came to mean scaring them.

The similarity between the roar of guns in a battle and the roar of the wind in a gale has given us the phrase for a ship travelling extremely fast in a very strong wind: GOING GREAT GUNS.

The early Spanish explorers encountered very fierce whirling storms when they crossed the Atlantic and explored the American coast. They described them by combining the words for thunderstorm (*tronada*) and turning (*tornar*) to produce the word TORNADO.

In the 16th century the Spanish had a word *malacia* meaning literally 'bad wind' – in effect, 'no wind': bad weather for sailing ships, of course. Conversely, their word for 'good wind' was *bonacia*. This became a good-luck wish for their treasure ships setting sail across the Atlantic to and from the Americas, where they were plundering the Aztec and Inca civilizations. Before long the word was being used to wish good luck to prospectors mining for gold, and it then became associated with successful prospectors who found rich seams of gold to mine – and then to any lucky strike or discovery, as a BONANZA.

The prefix 'a-' used to be added to the front of a word to add the meaning 'on'. Hence a ship stuck on land is AGROUND. A sailor going to a lofty position on a mast is ALOFT.

Loef was an old Dutch word meaning 'windward'. Clearly a sailing ship cannot sail directly into the wind, but it can sail slightly away from the wind and tack from side to side to make way in a direction contrary to the wind. Hence a word developed for a ship that was on a windward course but keeping slightly away from the wind's direction. This phrase is now often used in a social sense where an individual is going in a similar direction to the rest of the team but remains somewhat separate from them, keeping ALOOF.

'Large' was a word used to describe a ship that was running with the wind because it would usually have all of its sails in use and would therefore look large. This sense of 'sailing free with the wind' also gave the expression referring to escaped criminals as being AT LARGE. A ship that was sailing as close into the wind as possible, i.e. beating windward, could do so only by having the ropes on the rigging very tight or CLOSE HAULED. Ships sailing into the wind in this way were said to be 'sailing by'. Different ships had different qualities, but those that were good at sailing in all conditions, whether with or against the wind, were said to be the best BY AND LARGE.

The word 'way' is used to describe a ship's movement through the water. When a ship starts its journey and its sails begin to pick up the wind, it is said to be UNDER WAY. When it is proceeding against the weather conditions it is MAKING WAY or MAKING HEADWAY. An extreme version of 'making way' is when the whole crew is working very hard by tacking in one direction and then the other against the wind and almost 'cheating' the wind. It is then said to be ON THE MAKE, from where we get the meaning of the phrase with its implication of cheating.

If one ship holds back to allow another through in front of it, it GIVES WAY.

When sailing into the wind it is usually necessary to tack. Timing the tacking and getting the direction correct is crucial, especially near land. Once it starts to go wrong it is easy to end up in completely the wrong place and potentially in a dangerous situation – ON THE WRONG TACK.

When ships in the English Channel were trying to sail out to the Atlantic Ocean they would often have to sail against a south-westerly prevailing wind. Beating against such a wind would sometimes create a speed of only 2–3 knots relative to the water. However, if the ship was going against a tide of 3–5 knots then it would actually be going the wrong way. Therefore, by sailing against the wind when the tide was going in a helpful direction and then anchoring while the tide went the other way, progress could be made, albeit frustratingly slowly. The phrase describing this process is now much more widely used: TIDING OVER.

When a ship has the wind blowing into its sails they billow out and the ship sails very fast. If another ship blocks the wind by sailing directly upwind of it, the leading ship's sails fall limp and the ship quickly loses speed. Thus we have a phrase meaning to remove the source of someone's strength, confidence or plan, TO TAKE THE WIND OUT OF HIS SAILS. In modern yacht racing there are rules to govern who can and cannot undertake this manoeuvre.

Well, I never knew that . . .
. . . if you sail against the wind, you might be taken aback

Sometimes a ship facing into the wind cannot make any headway or is even blown backwards – hence TO BE TAKEN ABACK.

To sail in a particular direction and to get the maximum speed from any given wind strength and direction it is necessary to adjust or 'trim' the sails, using the ropes that control them. This prevents inefficient flapping or billowing of sails, which reduces the ship's speed. TRIMMING ONE'S SAILS is now a phrase widely used to mean making adjustments for changing situations.

Ships travel fastest when sailing in the same direction as the wind. Hence the advice to SAIL BEFORE THE WIND or SAIL WITH THE WIND BEHIND YOU. Doing the opposite is hard work and difficult: so don't SAIL AGAINST THE WIND.

When ships do sail into the wind they need to be careful how they manoeuvre; if they try tacking at too daring an angle they could lose control, or in fierce seas even capsize. Hence a phrase meaning to be 'edgy' and controversial while just avoiding disaster or crossing the line beyond acceptability, SAILING CLOSE TO THE WIND.

Under good conditions, the more sails a ship has the faster it will go. Hence the phrase meaning going as fast as one is able: UNDER FULL SAIL – and, by extension, the steam-age equivalents UNDER FULL STEAM and FULL STEAM AHEAD.

When steam engines were first used on ships the power was initially transferred to the water by large rotating wheels made of long wooden paddles; hence they were called PADDLE STEAMERS. For sea travel these wheels were placed one on each

side of the hull. There was more wheel out of the water than in the water, and so the top of the wheels was much higher than the deck. On some ships, basic decking with handrails was used to bridge the distance between the tops of the wheels to make it easier to get around and maintain the vessel. This actually provided a very good viewpoint and over the years became a lookout point, and then a cabin area from which the ship was controlled: THE BRIDGE.

When steam engines were first introduced to power ships, circular pieces of hemp were used as compression seals at the joints. These resembled circles of rope on masts called *garcettes* and over time the word evolved into GASKET.

When two sailing ships accidentally came too close to each other, so that their rigging or yardarms became entangled, they were said to be 'fouling' each other. Hence the expression meaning that two people have fallen into a quarrel, either by design or, more usually, by accident: FALLING FOUL OF EACH OTHER.

Nautically speaking, a 'sheet' is a rope used to trim a sail and the piece of the sail to which it is attached. If it is too loose, the sail flaps around madly, making the ship difficult to control. When this happens, to some extent the ship is under the control of the wind and is said to be IN THE WIND. Should more than one sheet be too loose or, even worse, if a storm rips the sails away from the ropes so that the sails are flapping and flailing in the wind, the ship becomes extremely difficult to control with even more haphazard movements. The terminology has been applied to being intoxicated: THREE SHEETS TO THE WIND.

When a galleon was sailing in a storm with a following sea, the rear (or poop) deck would often get flooded or overwhelmed by the sea – POOPED.

By analogy with a plant, the front part of a ship's hull was sometimes referred to as the 'stem'. Hence the expression describing a whole ship, FROM STEM TO STERN, and the phrase used when a ship is trying to sail against a tide and to keep the ship pointing into the tide, TO STEM THE TIDE – now used to mean fighting against the direction that something would go in if just left to itself.

When there is no wind a sailing vessel cannot control its movements and just drifts in the current, as a dead body would. It is DEAD IN THE WATER and the lack of breeze is called DEAD CALM. Interestingly, the word 'dead' developed a meaning of 'complete' or 'exact', from which we get the phrases for a sudden halt (DEAD STOP), hitting something exactly in the middle (DEAD CENTRE), and a slight variant in the timing of motor engines, the point at which a camshaft lifts a piston to its highest point (TOP DEAD CENTRE).

The French sailors' cry 'Help me!' has been adopted, in an anglicized version, for the international call for assistance: *M'aidez!* or, nowadays, MAYDAY. The earliest agreed international call sign was 'CQD', standing for 'COME QUICKLY – DANGER!' However, in 1908 it was decided to change it to a more memorable and distinctive call sign, SOS – SAVE OUR SOULS.

Klippa was an old Viking word meaning 'to pinch'. Hence we get the word for a device designed to 'pinch' together sheets of paper, a CLIP – and the related 'clipboard'. If you pinch something too tightly with a sharp clip you can actually tear or cut a piece off; hence a word evolved for a cutting tool, a CLIPPER. By medieval times the word 'clip' was being used to describe cutting something that was difficult to cut. When a new and very fast type of galleon was designed for rushing the new harvest of tea leaves back from India to England it was given very sharp bows designed to 'cut' through the water, and so these ships were called TEA CLIPPERS. The most famous of all the tea clippers is the *Cutty Sark*. From this association with very fast travel we get the phrase meaning to travel quickly, to CLIP ALONG. Nowadays 'clip' is associated with cutting small pieces off the main item, so in a beauty salon you get 'hair clippers' and 'nail clippers', and in a

workshop for trimming metal 'metal clippers' and 'wire clippers'. Interestingly, the word 'clippers' is still mainly used where the process of cutting actually involves some element of 'pinching'. **WINKT!**

6

Nelson, Our National Hero

Who better to round off this
maritime tour of the English
language than our national hero
and the victor of Trafalgar!

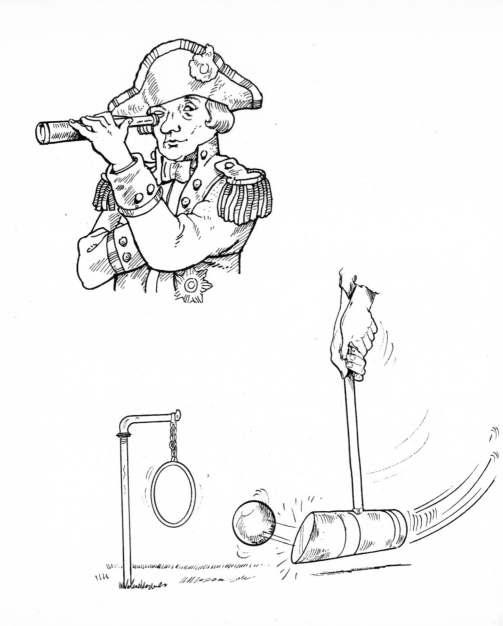

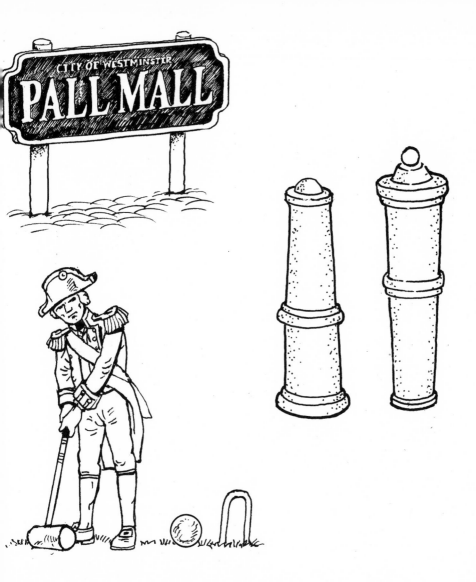

Well, I never knew that . . .
. . . Nelson thought Trafalgar would be a game of croquet
– and is still doing his national service!

In 1801 Nelson commanded a group of ships at the Battle of Copenhagen. An officer informed Nelson that the Admiral of the Fleet, Sir Hyde Parker, had sent a message instructing Nelson to cease fighting. The order was sent by flag signals, and when it was received and read out to Nelson, with characteristic audacity he raised his telescope to his blind eye and said: 'By God, I see no signal' – and continued the action. Hence the phrase TURN A BLIND EYE, meaning that you know something is happening that in theory should be acted upon but in practice is best ignored. (Nelson had lost much of the sight in his right eye as the result of an explosion in 1794 during an attack he was mounting on the Corsican fortress of Calvi. The wound caused very little scarring and he never, in fact, wore an eye-patch!) Nelson's temerity was

rewarded with both victory in battle and hero-worship by the British people – adulation that would steadily build to its climax after his death at the Battle of Trafalgar in 1805, on the point of achieving the victory which once and for all defeated Napoleon's navy and put paid to his chances of invading Britain.

Copenhagen wasn't the first time Nelson had ignored a superior's order. At the Battle of Cape St Vincent in 1797 he had disregarded his admiral's instructions and mounted a bold attack on two enemy ships simultaneously. Laying his own vessel alongside a Spanish ship that had fouled the Spanish flagship the *San Joseph*, Nelson led his men across the first ship on to the second, capturing both. This approach became known as NELSON'S BRIDGE.

In 1805, at the very start of the Battle of Trafalgar, Nelson ordered a message to be sent to his fleet including the words 'England confides that every man shall do his duty'. However, the signal officer was concerned that the word 'confide' would have be to spelt out letter by letter, as no shorthand form of it existed in the signalling code book. He therefore suggested an alternative word, giving final form to the most famous naval signal ever sent: 'ENGLAND EXPECTS THAT EVERY MAN SHALL DO HIS DUTY.'

When Nelson briefed his captains before the Battle of Trafalgar he said that he expected the battle to be a real 'pell mell' – meaning a vicious, hard-hitting, slog of a fight. Where does this phrase come from, and how is it connected to shopping?

Back in the 16th century a game originated in Italy that was called *pallo a maglio* or 'ball to mallet'. It became very popular with the gentry of France, where it was called *paille mall*. In the 17th century the game made its way to Scotland, which had long had close links with France forged through their mutual hatred of England, and thence to England, the Scottish line of Stuart kings having inherited the English throne in 1603. In 1660 King Charles II built an area specifically for playing this game in St James's Park, London, and the road that went past it, where onlookers gathered to watch the King play, adopted the English name of the game: PALL MALL. Over time this whole area became very popular and fashionable for walking, and the name of the road

became strongly associated with relaxed strolling. So when another road was built nearby it was simply called THE MALL. And it is from this name that we get our word for a shopping area designed purely for walking around, i.e. without cars: a SHOPPING MALL.

Back to the game, then. In 'pall mall' – or 'pell mell', as it also came to be called – the mallets were similar to modern croquet mallets but with one end (or sometimes both ends) cut at an angle so that the ball would be raised into the air when struck, the idea being to hit it through a metal ring suspended a short distance off the ground. In the 19th century

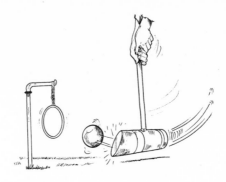

another version of pall mall evolved played with a different-shaped mallet that some people thought resembled a giant crochet hook – and so it was called CROQUET.

As with croquet today, the rules of pall mall enabled a skilful and aggressive player who could get his own ball through the hoops and hit other balls in the right order to take many shots in one turn and to progress around the playing area extremely quickly. From this aggressive winning strategy, and an association with the French word *mêlée*, we get the phrase meaning an aggressive and fast-moving fight, PELL MELL.

Hence Nelson's prediction – which of course turned out to be correct!

While the Battle of Trafalgar prevented Napoleon from invading Britain, it was another ten years before he was finally defeated, at the Battle of Waterloo in June 1815. The period of the Napoleonic wars had been the most widespread conflict that the world had yet seen, involving all the major European powers and fighting across several continents. As a result it was referred to afterwards as THE GREAT WAR – until the horrors of the 1914–18 war emerged, when that conflict took over the title. Interestingly, it was only with the 1939–45 war that the title 'World War' emerged, with the 1914–18 'Great War' then being referred to as the FIRST WORLD WAR.

With the demobilization of forces across Europe after the end of the Napoleonic wars, many guns, especially cannons, became surplus to requirements. At the time there was a need to protect pedestrians in London from wayward carriage-drivers who would accidentally veer into people by the side of the road. It was decided to put up bollards to deter such behaviour, and cannon barrels, sunk into the ground upright, were ideal for the purpose. Some were inserted with the open end in the ground; others had the open end pointing up, but with a cannon ball wedged into the end to stop water collecting inside the barrel. Hence the SHAPE OF BOLLARDS throughout the city of London, and, with other towns copying the style, across much of Britain.

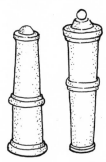

Nelson died at the very peak of his fame, popularity and career. The nation's joy at victory over the French and Spanish navies was diminished by the loss of such a national hero. In commemoration of the battle and in his honour, what is now one of the most famous squares in the world was dedicated to his success: TRAFALGAR SQUARE. Here, the four great bronze reliefs at the base of Nelson's Column that commemorate the Battles of Cape St Vincent, The Nile, Copenhagen and Trafalgar are all made from melted-down French cannon captured in his battles.

Less well known than Nelson's Column is a flotilla of model galleons that are still on the top of the gas lamps down each side of The Mall. This road connects Trafalgar Square to Buckingham Palace, and the ships represent the legacy of Nelson and the continuing work of the Royal Navy to protect the monarchy from its enemies. Nelson looks down upon these miniature galleons from the top of his column and so, not surprisingly, they are affectionately known as 'Nelson's Fleet'.

So incredibly, 200 years after the fateful battle of Trafalgar, and way beyond what England could expect – Nelson and his fleet are still doing their duty! WELL, I NEVER KNEW THAT! **WINKT!**

Thank you for reading this book. I do hope you said . . .

Please read on and find out about:

- Locating your favourite phrases from the Index.
- How you can help make a brand new word.
- How to join WINKT the club.
- Other fascinating books in the series.
- 'Houston – we MAY have a problem'.
- How to discover your family's history, coat of arms and the origin of your surname.

Index

MESSAGE FROM THE AUTHOR

Please help create a brand new word!

'Well I Never Knew That!' – the story so far

Back in Victorian Dublin a man bet that he could get everyone in Dublin using a brand new word within 24 hours. He won the bet by having four letters scrawled all over the walls that night. The next morning everyone pointed at the letters, said them out loud and said, 'What is that?' The letters were Q U I Z. He had created the word QUIZ, which we now use to describe competitions where someone says – 'What is …?'

I foolishly made a similar bet in a pub – to create a brand new word and to get it into the dictionary. This turned into a gargantuan project of tracking down and linking the most intriguing, fascinating and funniest origins of everyday phrases and names in the English language. All the boring ones have been thrown away! That's how this series of books came about!

When friends read the first book they often said 'Well, I never knew that!' – hence the name of the series. Then they shortened it to WINKT – the acronym of 'Well I Never Knew That!' meaning 'Wow!' or 'Gosh!' This is the new word: 'WINKT'!!!

'Please help finish the story!'

Now you've got WINKT the book – why not help create 'WINKT' the word and finish the story! All you have to do is send an email to word@winkt.com saying that 'I think "WINKT", meaning "Wow!" or "Gosh!" should be a new word in the dictionary.'

This will be added to the petition and when we get enough you will have played your part in creating a BRAND NEW WORD in the English language! In fact, if we get more than enough, we may even get into the *Guinness Book of World Records* as the most requested word ever! And, of course, tell your friends to email in as well. The more the merrier!

As a thank you I will give you free membership of WINKT the club!
Thank you,

Now you have enjoyed a WINKT book why not join WINKT the club?

As a member you can benefit from:

- Advance information on new books before they are generally available.

- Information on other WINKT products, cards, posters, etc.

- Beautiful manuscript-style scrolls that tell the professionally researched history and heritage of your family surname together with an historically accurate full-colour coat of arms. Fascinating and eye-catching presents, either framed or unframed. We can also offer a scroll with two coats of arms – ideal for a wedding or anniversary present.

- The opportunity to get your name into the credits of a future WINKT book by offering a new WINKT expression.

- A newsletter with more fascinating derivations, members' questions, competitions and prizes.

- Occasional emails sent to you with fascinating new WINKT origins.

- Sets of approved WINKT questions for use in pub/trivia quizzes, parties or dinner parties.

- 'Ask Peter' service for the derivation of specific words or phrases.

- Join the campaign to get 'WINKT' recognized as an official word and enter the Guinness Book of World Records to get the most requested word ever!

And much, much more.

Simply register online at www.WINKT.com and get your friends and family to register too! Join the fun today!

Recommended questions for Book Circles

'Well, I Never Knew That!' books are great for book circles because they can be read a little bit at a time, are such fun and always spark off interesting questions and discussions that can cause a real stir! For example:

- Which origins most surprised you?
- Which was your most 'WINKTASTIC' moment?
- How many times did you actually say 'Well, I never knew that!'?
- Who have you shared the WINKTs with and what was their reaction?
- How many times have you noticed people using the phrases since reading the book?
- What regional or family variations in phrases have you noticed?
- What must it be like for foreigners trying to learn English?
- What phrases or expressions used by other people really annoy you?
- What different nicknames do you use for family/friends or human anatomy?
- What phrases have been used in your family for years without anyone ever challenging what they really mean or why they exist?
- What new words or phrases do children bring back from school?
- What other phrases do you now want to know the origin of?

You can always log on to www.winkt.com and simply 'Ask Peter'.

And of course if you know a really interesting origin let Peter know so he can include it in a future book and include your name in the credits!

We love hearing from book circles and so, as a thank you, we offer special discounts for book-club orders. Log on to www.winkt.com to find out more.

Other books in the WINKT series

DID NOAH INVENT TENNIS?

AN HISTORIC MISCELLANY

Do you know ...

... why we score tennis 'love, 15, 30, 40, deuce'?

... why you had better 'cut to the chase', to avoid running 'from pillar to post'?

... why getting the 'sack' is better than being 'fired'?

... why the Battle of Agincourt was such a 'cock-up' for the French?

... why the 'exception' doesn't 'prove the rule' – and never did!

ISBN 0-9551525-1-8
ISBN 978-0-9551525-1-1

THE HISTORY OF GREAT BRITAIN

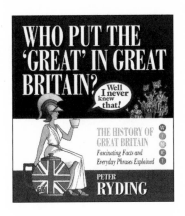

Do you know ...

... why England has three heraldic lions – because none of them was English!

... why Cromwell was such a 'whitewash', 'warts and all'?

... why we call our flag a 'Union JACK' – and why you may never have seen one?

... why a popular nursery rhyme teaches our children about destruction, boozing, pawning and child mortality? It's enough to make you 'pop your clogs'!

... and what is a 'cock-horse' anyway?

ISBN 0-9551525-3-4
ISBN 978-0-9551525-3-5

SPORTS, GAMES AND GAMBLING

Do you know ...

... why going 'down like ninepins' may get you 'knocked into a cocked hat'?

... why we train Olympic athletes to be spies?

... why we call football 'soccer'?

... how you can play cards with Alexander the Great and Julius Caesar?

... why 'passing the buck' is not a 'good idea'?

ISBN 0-9551525-6-9
ISBN 978-0-9551525-6-6

DID ROMANS DESIGN THE SPACE SHUTTLE?

THE ROMAN EMPIRE

Do you know ...

... how the Romans 'made a mint' when their city was destroyed?

... why they didn't just have vandals – they virtually invented them?

... how Roman sewers have helped specify modern trains and the Space Shuttle?

... why anyone paid a 'salary' owes it all to the Romans – especially if they are not 'worth their salt'?

... why the Romans gave us 'malaria'?

ISBN 0-9551525-5-0
ISBN 978-0-9551525-5-9

WHAT EVER HAPPENED TO OUR 27TH LETTER?

KNOWLEDGE, AND HOW WE USE IT!

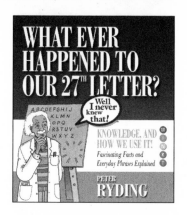

Do you know ...

... which flag gave bakers 13 to a dozen?

... why we all end sentences in Latin without even knowing it?

... what is the 27th letter of our alphabet?

... which idiot created fool's-cap paper and when did it become 'stationery'?

... how come the Sumerians gave us nothing but changed the world for ever?

ISBN 0-9551525-7-7
ISBN 978-0-9551525-7-3

Future WINKT books for release in 2007 and 2008

Log on to www.winkt.com to find out more.
Join the club and receive advance information of new releases!

- Time, Astronomy and Astrology
- Food and Drink
- London and Londoners
- Knights and Warfare through the Ages
- Big Business and Great Brands

- Ancient Greece
- USA and the World
- Cockney Rhyming Slang
- and more!

You've read the book – now play the game!

WELL I NEVER KNEW THAT – THE ADVENTURE!

The fun and fast-moving interactive **DVD** and **TV GAME** with fascinating and intriguing pictures, photos and video clues.

10 games on a DVD disc – guaranteed no repeat questions.

The perfect gift for lovers of words, phrases, history and our national heritage.

Available from www.winkt.com Autumn 2006.

Also by the same author

'Houston – we MAY have a problem!'

How to spot business issues early and fix them.

ISBN 0-9551525-9-3
ISBN 978-0-9551525-9-7

Copies can be ordered from www.peterryding.com

*'I commend this book to anyone who feels they MAY be facing business challenges …
amusing and entertaining but without pulling any punches.'*

SIR JOHN HARVEY-JONES MBE (of TV *Troubleshooter* fame)

*'This short book is the most straightforward and digestible piece of commercial
education that I have come across.'*

CHIEF EXECUTIVE OF THE SOCIETY OF TURNAROUND PROFESSIONALS

In the fast-paced business world of today everyone is under more stress than ever before. That includes CEOs and their directors. No wonder they need help. But how and when should they get that help?

This book provides the answer in a very short, illustrated and highly readable way. It is written by one of the UK's leading profit improvement experts and is specifically for CEOs and their leadership teams.

It tells the story of John, a CEO with a problem.

The trouble is, it has crept up on him and he doesn't know what to do.

'King Harold is too busy to see any salesmen right now.'

In fact, he doesn't really understand the severe implications for his business and for himself personally.

He then does the first of three critical things.

He gets help.

But is it too late?

If you haven't been there before, it is very tough to spot the problem, to identify which levers to pull, to know whom to believe and how to manage the various stakeholders around you. This book shows you what to do and what not to do.

'Reading this book could be the best spent thirty minutes of your career and save you a lot more than your job!'

SIR DIGBY JONES, DIRECTOR GENERAL OF THE CBI

To contact Peter please email peter@pathfinderpro.co.uk

Surname History and Coat of Arms

Do you know the origin of your surname?
Do you know the history of your family name from the middle ages?
Do you know the coat of arms or motto associated with it?
We do!

We specialize in providing professionally researched backgrounds to surnames and first names including coat of arms where relevant.

We can provide beautiful manuscript-style scrolls either framed or unframed.

We can provide two coats of arms side by side for a special wedding or anniversary present.

We can even provide the history of a friend's or relative's first name and surname for a very personal and treasured historical gift.

Log on to www.WINKT.com and order yours now!